Everything's Be Cool!

6 Personal Development Lessons to Elevate Your Workplace Vibe

By

Hanan Harb Sahourieh

Dedications

This book is dedicated to my incredible late mother, **Nahida**, my husband, **Jacob**, and my children, **Zoey Nahida** and **Jirius Jacob.**

And to all the people out there dedicated to **making the world better, kinder, and cooler**. Thank you. We need you. Keep going.

Acknowledgments

Tiffany Vojnovski aka Liege O' Lieges aka Waldorf
Dr. Alamira Reem al Hashimi
Professor Mays Danfoura
Professor James Holstun
Farid and Tamam Harb
Maria and Eddy Khawaja
Irene Lewis
Barnes & Noble, bookstores, libraries, and safe spaces around the world
Elizabeth Leiba
Lauren Richardson-Berg
Christina Dyer
Meredith Farley
Isabel Sterne
Grace Redman
Neha Mandhani
Tiffany Totah
Alethea O'Dell
Cher Jones
Ellen Gillis
Joelle Jackson
Robert Jackson
Arsalan al Hashimi
Esther Lejano
Team Maté
Jai White
Deepti Bhadkamkar
Pansy Romo

Table of Contents

Introduction

To paraphrase *Mean Girls*, raise your hand if you've been personally **victimized by the workplace**!

Cue: the entire world raising their hands in unison.

And if you *haven't* been personally victimized by the workplace, congratulations! I'm about to share the once-guarded secrets reserved for corporate executives...but you're OK with me sharing because you're cool, right?

I thought so! You seem cool. You know there can be room for us all to thrive.

Here's the thing…

Any time humans come together, they form groups and hierarchies. And things can get **intense**. Especially when *money, identity, and status* are involved, which human beings take <u>very</u> seriously. The stakes are high!

Often, the work that takes up most of our energy is dealing with *workplace dysfunction*. It can manifest as **communication, conflict, and/or cultural** issues. An entire industry of professional coaches rose to prominence because so many employees need additional support to deal with emotions in the workplace.

Many people in the workforce struggle in a system that drains and burns them out. The workplace encourages employees to be "themselves"…But not *too much*. Just the right amount of themselves that depends on leadership's oftentimes arbitrary perception of them. There's no way to know for sure what "be yourself" means in any given situation.

My manager at my first post-college job told me in a testy exchange, "If there's one thing you need to know in life, it's that your manager needs to like you." It was an incredibly awkward and traumatizing encounter for my early-20s self. I remember thinking, "Well, I didn't know you didn't like me, but I guess I know now!"

Weirdly, she was right. If your manager doesn't like you, it sucks. And that happens. Not everyone will like you. You may find that **your mere existence triggers people**. Even if you deliver on the <u>actual work</u>.

A lot of the workplace is a social dance. Sometimes, it's the macarena and, sometimes, it's a mosh pit. Often, you don't know the steps until you've tripped and fallen over and over again.

Prospective employees are scared to enter a workforce that is a major source of stress to their parents' generation. The new workforce is demanding things like *flexibility and working remotely*. The intense "sleep when you're dead" mentality from the '80s and '90s is no longer being rewarded, thankfully. Employees are yearning to reclaim their time and their peace of mind—even when the job market is weird and erratic (which it usually is).

So, why did I decide to write this book?

I've been intrigued by the workplace since before I entered it. Like many of us, work played an integral role in changing my family's fate. My eldest uncle, Farid, was the first of our family to emigrate to America in the 1950s, looking for safety, freedom, and opportunity. He worked his way up in Bethlehem Steel—a giant factory in its day. Farid's strong work ethic, grit, and determination helped him move up through the ranks of the iconic and now-defunct factory that helped build America.

Later in life and long retired, my uncle regaled me with stories of how he worked his way from sweeping in the factory to an elevated task with a small increase in pay and responsibilities. Little by little, he was promoted. He said his co-workers told him to slow down because he was making them look bad in comparison. But he didn't. He kept working as hard as possible, reaping incremental raises and rewards. He was proud of himself for being able to buy a nice home in a nice neighborhood after many years of working hard and saving up.

Each of Farid's brothers left their homeland to relocate and join him to chase the elusive American Dream. My dad was the face of Mr. Softee, a mobile ice cream truck franchise, while my mom was able to focus solely on raising her family.

My family's strength, resilience, and determination inspired me to do the sensible, hardworking thing and become a doctor or a pharmacist, encouraged by my older pharmacist cousin. So, I gave it a shot. That lasted exactly *five minutes* into my first and last Organic Chemistry class in college! I quickly realized the pharmacist route was not for me.

Even though my family's approach to work inspired me, I couldn't just "grit and determine" my way through a subject that instantly made my brain feel numb—*shoutout to doctors and science people*! I gave up on the pipe dream quickly and got realistic. Instead, I followed my **love of words**, *feeeelingsssss*, critical thinking, and unpacking the meaning of things. I became an English Literature major! I never had a clear plan of what to do after college or a basic understanding of my career options. I just knew I loved reading and writing and hoped things would fall into place when I graduated.

Workplace Vibes

I found my first post-graduation job by applying to every job with the word "writer." That's how I began my career as a technical writer.

When I entered the workplace post-college, I found myself in spaces where I felt clueless, surrounded by people who seemed to "understand the rules." I knew how to dissect the symbolism in Shakespeare but not much about working in an office with all different types of human beings as a confused 22-year-old.

I began my career with a textbook case of **imposter phenomenon or syndrome**. There was no manual. There was just Fight-or-Flight survival mode. My main desired outcome/driving factor was: **"Don't get fired."**

I focused on how much *I didn't know*, thinking I missed the presentation on "how things work." It was a classic **scarcity mindset**. I didn't realize how much the workplace entailed navigating others' emotions and personalities. I didn't realize I could empower myself through communication and conflict-resolution skills.

Since then, I've worked for hyper-growth companies, billion-dollar companies, global companies, and everything in between. I'd be lying if I said the road has been easy. There was no blueprint. I've grown my career path as a writer, learning professional, and marketer working for world-renowned brands. I've met amazing people and learned many lessons along the way.

Co-Workers and Workplace BFFs

What's the common denominator in the workplace? **People.** Some co-workers in the workplace **communicate** well. Some do *not*. Some co-workers **manage their emotions** well. Some do *not*.

I've made great friends in the workplace in my career—BFFs (best friends forever) even. That's how I became *Your Workplace BFF*, author of the **Workplace Matters** newsletter, which explores **elevating the vibe** at work and life. I wanted to hype people up in the workplace and promote love and togetherness.

Over late-night drinks, honest one-on-one lunches, or dinners with friends and colleagues around the country, I've had the honor to connect with many diverse, intelligent, empathetic people who felt gaslit, hurt, or both by the workplace. They trusted me to share their authentic selves, concerns, hopes, and frustrations.

I noticed that incredibly smart, empathetic, and motivated people are **routinely overlooked and judged unfairly** in the workplace. Maybe they didn't know how to "play the corporate politics" game or hype themselves up enough to be seen how they wanted to be seen. Maybe they thought they would be recognized if they put their head down and focused on the work.

*Spoiler alert: **They didn't.***

These workplace BFFs worked at companies lauded as case studies in cultural excellence. Even places that were awarded "best places to work." And while they were, in fact, awesome in many ways and employed amazing people, there were many *stressful* and *toxic* aspects to navigating those workplaces and conflicting personalities that were all vying to ascend to power (while also totally being "a family here").

Confusion, frustration, ego battles, and roadblocks in the workplace are a reality for human beings from all walks of life. There's been an obsession with leaders in recent years…but what about **individual contributors—the glue of the workplace**? I wanted to share perspectives from those doers who have been in the workplace trenches churning out work and those who are guiding how it's evolving.

Being stuck in your career was not supposed to be the reward for keeping your head down and working hard, especially after excelling at school and collecting your gold stars. Being nice, working well with others, and following the rules worked in school, but does it translate in the workplace? The transition from school to the workplace can shock many of us. Especially when the workplace doesn't have set rules and the unspoken rules tend to differ wildly from one person to the next.

Why and How This Book Came to Be

When I got laid off in the summer of 2023, I realized this was my chance to do something I've wanted to do since I was a child. Time to write a book! It felt like a sign from the universe. I was frustrated that I wasn't getting the opportunities that I thought I deserved. So, I **gave myself a promotion** to author and spent half a year researching and writing.

Some common **frustrations** people have in the workplace include:
- *Why were others picked for leadership development programs and not me?*
- *How could I get others to recognize my talent or contributions?*
- *Why do I have to tiptoe around others' toxic traits?*
- *What would it take to move my career forward?*

That's exactly why I wrote <u>this</u> book.

I wrote this book for:

- The people pleasers (or reforming people pleasers) who don't want to wait passively for the magical, hypothetical day when their hard work and talent finally get recognized.

- The people who are overlooked, undervalued, and never had the inside scoop on how to "make it."

- Those of us who never had a mentor or sponsor to show us the ropes or advocate for us behind closed doors.

- Those of us who have been judged unfairly and not given the opportunities that help our careers grow.

- For anxious people who sweat their way through each day.

Many are sweating right alongside you in solidarity. I wrote this book to share the insights that may be overlooked by the standard business books that focus on *"Leading Leaders Who Lead."* As we've seen globally, **leaders often do <u>not</u> have all the answers**. Sometimes, they're completely misguided. Sometimes, they're destructive. After all, they are human.

As an individual contributor in the Learning & Development and Content Marketing spaces, I saw a disproportionate emphasis on **leadership development** in the workplace. However, "doers" far outnumber leaders and managers in the workplace.

What about the specialists in the workplace? What tools and pathways are there? I want to share the personal development secrets that have been saved for leadership development programs with employees in the workplace who are still carving their paths.

So, I dove into the workplace from an individual's perspective. I spoke with **executive coaches, branding specialists, LinkedIn experts, learning and marketing professionals, spiritual teachers, and experienced leaders**. Many said that much of the workplace is navigating *communication issues, mental health issues, and office politics.* I also devoured **teachings on spirituality as well as research and best practices in personal development and the workplace**.

I was determined to answer the question: *How can individuals in the workplace empower themselves, no matter their role or organization?*

People in the workplace don't need another yoga or meditation webinar—they need a tool to help **elevate their consciousness**. I'm sharing all I've learned with you and my experience creating learning and development programs for world-renowned companies and as a marketer.

You don't have to wait to get promoted or selected for a leadership development program to start the journey of personal development. *Why wait to start elevating ourselves?*

Now is the time. No more gatekeeping. This book is your ticket. I hope to democratize the workplace by sharing the **existential insights** and **self-development tools** reserved for leadership with everyone interested in growing and evolving. We can do this. You got this!

"You get a personal development secret! And <u>YOU</u> get a personal development secret!"

Sure, a lot of the onus can be placed on **management and leadership** in the workplace, but every single one of us affects the whole. A toxic workplace or individuals can counteract all of our personal development. When your reality is the stark opposite of the utopia "family" that is being falsely promised, this can lead to more toxicity in a cycle of frustration and defeat. Life is always hard. Even when it's good. That's why this is a lifelong practice—hate to break it to you. But it can be fun!

If we commit to **elevating ourselves** and each other, we all benefit.

This is a **personal and professional development book** with spiritual and workplace strategies curated from best practices in coaching, leadership, learning & development, and content marketing. You'll find several **Spiritual Business Moments** throughout the book. We can't address how we show up at work without addressing how we see the world. Introspection helps you deeply examine who you are to help you access what you need to thrive in your environment.

Are you where you want to be? What can you do to look at things differently? How can you best deal with this complex, stressful, and messy world?

What adjustments could you make to adjust your perspective and make your life—and those around you—<u>better</u>?

Cool: From the Individual to the Collective

Being **cool** in the workplace means that you:
- Make others feel comfortable
- Are transparent with their intentions
- Are curious
- Listen to others
- Care about others' lived experiences
- Are open to perspectives they may have never considered
- Change their mind when new information is presented
- Practice what they preach
- Check in with themselves
- Say what they mean and mean they say
- Want to see others succeed
- Are collaborative

If that's what you want to see in the workplace, change starts with you. It's been suggested that **we're all different parts of the same being** from a metaphysical perspective.

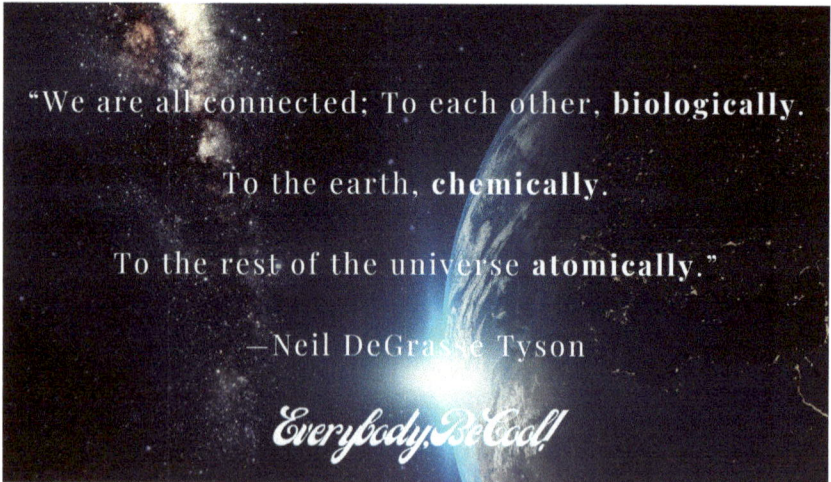

"We are all connected: To each other, **biologically**.

To the earth, **chemically**.

To the rest of the universe **atomically**."

—Neil DeGrasse Tyson

Everybody Be Cool!

I believe the previous quote from **Neil DeGrasse Tyson** deeply in my soul. **We are all connected.** (Read that again). Whether we want to believe that or not, we are all on this planet as part of the same ecosystem. We're all playing a role and we affect each other more than we realize.

Spiritual Business Moment: When we fight each other, we fight ourselves on a larger level. Despite the labels we put on ourselves or others. Despite the "othering" we do to people we don't understand. You could be "that person" in an alternate reality. What would you do if you were reincarnated in a less fortunate position? Would that change your current perspective?

According to *Merriam-Webster*, **vibration** is defined as: "a characteristic emanation, aura, or spirit that infuses or vitalizes someone or something and that can be instinctively sensed or experienced—often used in plural." Scientifically speaking, the vibes in the early 2020s have been "toilet garbage." I hope to **elevate the collective vibration** in the workplace and beyond with this book.

I want to help people move from *sadness, fear, anger, separation, and competition* to **care, community, connection, and joy**.

In addition, I hope to give you a **roadmap for your personal and professional development**. Professional development and personal development are different ways of saying the same thing. *The end result?* It will enrich your life all around.

The journey of personal development can help beyond your career and can ignite a transformative voyage that reaches far beyond you. It touches the hearts and minds of those around you, creating a collective vibration of **resilience, innovation, and even love**.

When you develop yourself, this **enlightenment** transcends the workplace and impacts families, communities, and the world. It's an awareness that you are connected to everything around you. And you create a collective "vibe," which can be **workplace culture**, your local community, and any group you're a part of.

In this new paradigm, the workplace can spark change, causing a ripple effect that creates **a better, more compassionate world** beyond its walls. **Elevating the vibe** in the workplace requires each of us. And it's important to cultivate our vibe, no matter where we are in our lives and careers.

The more clear our perspective, the more we can navigate any situation.

In this book, there are 6 personal development lessons to help you navigate any workplace.

1. Be aware of your surroundings.

2. Journey into your awareness.

3. Improve your communication.

4. Understand your conflict style.

5. Manage your expectations.

6. Be your own workplace BFF.

The six lessons and tools found in this book will help you heal, create positive interactions with others, and solve complex challenges. You have the power to elevate the collective vibration, starting with yourself. It's not leaders; it's everyone in the workplace.

Take back your power, **create the reality that you want to see,** and level up.

Get your pen or pencil handy (yes, old-school) if you're reading a physical copy of this book. There will be **self-reflective exercises in each chapter**.

Get ready to develop and empower yourself, get unstuck, and elevate your vibe and professional presence…and have some stinkin' fun in the process! Embrace the journey!

This work is the pathway to a workplace—and a world—transformed. Just be cool, everybody.

Let's goooooo.

Lesson #1: Be aware of your surroundings.

What's the Context?

It's easy to look around at **unrest, incivility, oppression, genocide, and other bad vibes** in the world and think that our times are *uniquely bad*. But here's some reassuring news: the world has always been horrifying! Just in ways unique to the historical moment.

Recall the Inquisition in the 1200s? The Plague—also known as the Black Death—in the 1300s? Wars throughout history?

Super, super unchill.

We may have deluded ourselves that we've grown or evolved since The Middle Ages, but that's not really the case.

"At least it's not the Inquisition" could be an interesting mantra for the 2020s. Of course, there are great things, achievements, love, progress, understanding, **true empathy**—*not the fake corporate kind but legit empathy*—connection, elevated consciousness, and everything else between these catastrophic events.

And for every humanity-destroying, power-hungry sociopath we see in history (and the present), there are many others who are kind, loving, helpful, and committed to moving humanity forward. The dance of push and pull continues in different forms.

Everything is cyclical. Everything is a pattern.

The players change but we all, as a society, engage in a similar dance through the ages. We like to convince ourselves that the time we're living in is somehow unique, but it's just a *variation of that pattern.*

Feel better?

I didn't think so, but **context** always helps you understand where you are. It empowers you. Without context, it's like starting a movie in the middle. The same is true of any space you occupy, whether *familial, religious, communal, societal, political, or global.* Wherever you are, you need to **be aware of your surroundings and the context of the space you're holding**. That means where you are now and what came before you.

We like to think we're evolved, but we're not. I would be lying if I said I wasn't depressed and disheartened by the state of the world. I grew up being told that the world got better over time and that people would never allow atrocities to happen like they did in "olden times." That people would never stand for injustice.

That's simply not true. It happens time and time again and people are gaslit into thinking that it's somehow justifiable.

We would hope that we know or do better <u>now</u>, but that's not the case, as author, historian, and activist **Howard Zinn** reminds us in the following quote.

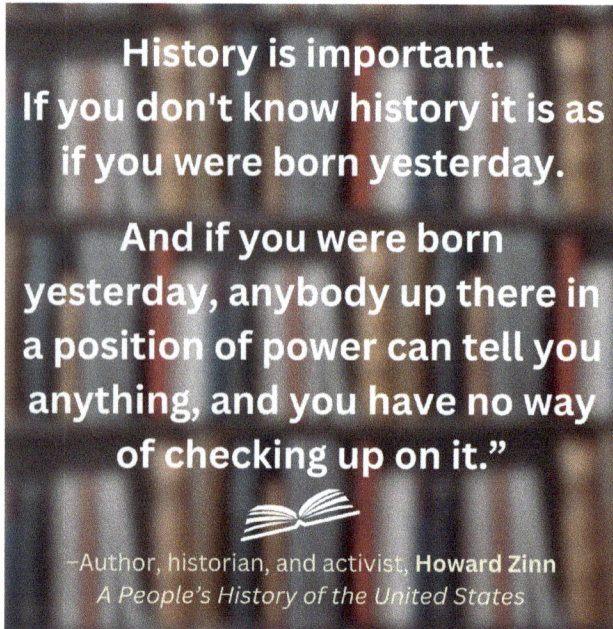

> **History is important.**
> **If you don't know history it is as**
> **if you were born yesterday.**
>
> **And if you were born**
> **yesterday, anybody up there in**
> **a position of power can tell you**
> **anything, and you have no way**
> **of checking up on it."**
>
> –Author, historian, and activist, **Howard Zinn**
> *A People's History of the United States*

Workplace Patterns

Everything's constantly in flow, especially in the workplace. Daily deadlines, Zoom calls, emails, instant messages, cranky co-workers trying to Lady Macbeth-power-play their way to the top, work BFFs, and everything in between (Shakespeare, 2003).

And in the **2020s,** employees are dealing with an onslaught of natural disasters, global horrors, and strife lurking in the background—all while trying to meet deadlines. And take walks. And do "self-care." And not lose their minds.

Employees are navigating a new terrifying headline or change in society at a rate that feels disproportionate to past generations. It's information overload. Many of us are coping with so many different traumas and changes. People are showing up to their workplace with fried nervous systems. *After all, the show must go on, right?* It's no wonder **burnout** is at an all-time high (Shoss, 2023)!

But it's not all doom and gloom. Therapist, coach, and entrepreneur **Christina Dyer** shares, "The world itself is in a *transformational shift* for the better. When you have a wound, you have to clean it out."

Since trends are cyclical, **knowledge is power for you in the workplace (and life)**. As each decade passes and a new generation starts working, the workplace *ebbs and flows* to reflect societal changes. A tale as old as time!

The workplace adapts and adjusts to its people and where they put their *energy*. That collective energy manifests new realities based on the **collective consciousness**, which is a concept first introduced in the late 1800s by French sociologist Émile Durkheim.

Collective consciousness is defined as "the body of beliefs and sentiments common to the average of members of a society."

Today's **Gen Z and Millennials** versus **Baby Boomers** battling out workplace values is not novel. It's playing out with the push and pull of: *"Don't make us come back to the office, boomer!"* versus *"You get your lazy butt back to the office and be productive, hippie!"*

There's *always* been friction between older and younger generations. There's always been norms being broken and those who want to stick with the comfort of the **status quo** without challenging existing beliefs.

This knowledge informs the present and can help you make more sense of the landscape you're in.

How did we get here?

Five generations comprise the workplace in the last century: **Silent, Baby Boomers, Gen X, Millennials, and Gen Z**. Gen Alpha are not old enough to enter the workplace yet—unless they're the occasional YouTuber who gets rich opening up Pokémon packs.

WORKPLACE (R)EVOLUTION TIMELINE

Shaping Each Decade

Generations—Silent to Alpha

1. **Silent: 1928 - 1945**
2. **Boomers: 1946 - 1964**
3. **Generation X: 1965 - 1980**
4. **Millennials: 1981 - 1996**
5. **Generation Z: 1997 - 2012**
6. **Generation Alpha: 2013 - 2023**

Each generation had its *traumas, influences, ideas,* and *breakthroughs.* **Look for the patterns** as you read about the decades and generations in this section. You'll notice a push and pull between generations—*old and new* (Loria, 2023).

Change versus the status quo. You'll also notice movements, philosophies, and values changing over time (and then changing back a decade or two later).

How did ideas evolve? Nothing stays stagnant. Pay attention to the trends and new technology that influenced the times.

Early 1900s

If you think the modern workplace is stressful, let's travel back **100 years**. In the early 1900s, workers faced long hours, poor working conditions, and job instability. There were many, many worker deaths due to a lack of safety standards.

Popular books in this era that reflect the overarching sense of danger and instability of the era include 1906's *The Jungle* by Upton Sinclair, which also became a film. *The Jungle* focused on the meat industry and depicts working-class poverty, lack of social support, harsh and unpleasant living and working conditions, and hopelessness among many workers of the time (Sinclair, 2019).

Both world wars impacted labor markets significantly and global unrest dominates this time period. World War II, in particular, actually created **millions of jobs for women** (Atlassian.com, 2020). A *physical safety revolution* resulted in **major systemic changes**. Workers pushed for changes that addressed the dangerous working conditions in mines, railroads, factories, farms, and more. The **Silent Generation** was born (quietly, we can presume by the name). And thankfully, in the early 1900s, government agencies and corporations started to establish voluntary safety programs as well as **child labor laws in the United States**.

Hurray! No kids in the workplace, please. It's bad enough when you have to deal with a grown adult who acts like a toddler. As challenging as work can be, you can always be thankful you're not a child working in a factory. *Bright side?*

After meeting some basic physiological and safety needs, the workplace ascended on **Maslow's Hierarchy of Needs** (Mcleod, n.d.). According to the famous psychological pyramid, once you meet the more basic bottom needs, you can start meeting the more complicated needs towards the top.

THE ROAD TO SELF-ACTUALIZATION (MASLOW'S HIERARCHY)

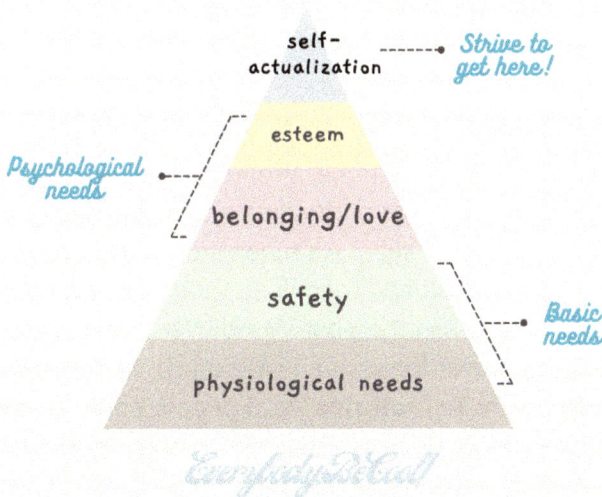

self-actualization ------• *Strive to get here!*

esteem

Psychological needs ---

belonging/love

safety ----• *Basic needs*

physiological needs

EverybodyBChill

Dale Carnegie's bestselling book *How to Win Friends & Influence People* emphasized the importance of interpersonal workplace skills. It went on to become one of the best-selling books of all time.

The self-help book was based on Carnegie's 14-week courses on human relations and public speaking, and some of its teachings are still relevant today.

Some lessons/rules from the iconic book include:

- "Become genuinely interested in other people."
- "Smile!"
- "The only way to get the best of an argument is to avoid it."
- "Let the other person feel that the idea is his or hers" (Carnegie, 1998).

We weren't quite there yet with the whole **interpersonal awareness** thing and nowhere near Maslow's concept of transcendence, but *baby steps, workplace…baby steps.*

1950s

In the '50s, Baby Boomers joined the planet, and the **Silent Generation** joined the workforce. Workers could expect better physical safety and more opportunities and industries during this time than the prior generation. As mass industrial automation took off, factory jobs declined and machines took over the manual workplace. Employees in the post-World War II workforce could focus on gaining power through an **office job, rather than long, often unsafe hours in factories**. And people could smoke in the office too!

This is when many immigrants—like my Uncle Farid—came to America looking to build a life for themselves and their families with a few dollars in their pockets, a lot of heart, and a strong work ethic. They escaped from strife, persecution, and a lack of opportunities to run towards a new life called "The American Dream."

Writers like Ayn Rand (*boooo hisss*) influenced the 1950s. Rand popularized the **dog-eat-dog** business philosophy with her book *Atlas Shrugged*. Her "ethical egoism" philosophy encouraged *selfishness and productivity* above all else, opposing altruism.

!!!

So, essentially, that generation was told that their greatest achievement as human beings is their **productivity**? Yikes. Okay, well, that explains A LOT.

1950s Books

Moving away from factory norms, the post-war office workplace ushered in a new reality and expectations for American workers. Yet, office layouts were modeled after the factory floor as desks were crammed tightly together. The technology of the day included manual typewriters and adding machines. Elliott Jaques first introduced the concept of **corporate culture** in 1951's *The Changing Culture of a Factory,* a case study of factory operations.

The message from this era seems to be: *"Keep producing and conforming, people!"* It would take a while (even a few generations) before the workplace moved away from treating the office like a human factory with people expected to fall in line with uniformity like manufactured products on a conveyor belt.

1950s Media

1950s TV shows like *Leave It to Beaver* presented the archetypal family structure of the time with a working father, stay-at-home mother, and kids. It's a trope often looked at with nostalgia for its portrayal of simpler times and suburban bliss.

The *"gee, ain't life swell"* facade also covered a repressive environment built on tensions that resulted from The Cold War and McCarthysim.

My family's reality, like millions of others, looked different. There was no *Leave It to Farid* at this point on TV although immigrants made the country what it is today. It didn't reflect what the "melting pot" actually looked like, just an idealized version of what was considered "The American Dream" at that time.

1960s

The conformity of the '50s made way for the rebellious, swingin' **'60s**, full of social upheaval and transformation.

In this era, the **Baby Boomer** generation entered the workforce. This generation pushes back on this idyllic *Leave it to Beaver* homogeneous message emphasizing uniformity. They wanted to be seen for who they were. And they wanted equal rights.

A worldwide series of political movements, known as **Civil Rights**, grew (Hamlin, 2024). The movement sought to ensure that all people are equally protected by the law. In 1964, the **Civil Rights Act** passed, which ended segregationist Jim Crow laws and promised that the workplace could not discriminate on race, religion, gender, or ethnicity (*Legal Highlight: The Civil Rights Act of 1964*, n.d.).

According to human resources business partner **Lauren Richardson-Berg**, "We still rely on the Civil Rights Act to this day in the workplace, and the Supreme Court still refers to it when it comes to discrimination."

The '60s also saw the **birth of the cubicle** when Robert Propst, a designer for Herman Miller, designed the *first modular desk system* (Drake Baer, 2014). But, did you know that its first release tanked? Herman Miller then released a cheaper follow-up, which is easy to install and ready for the growing number of middle management folks in corporate America. And cubicle history was made. Technological innovations include International Business Machines (IBM) electronic typewriters, improving typists' speed and productivity (Atlassian.com, 2020).

And would you believe me if I told you the U.S. Army invented **soft skills** in the late '60s? Sort of! Not necessarily invented, but named. The army coined the phrase to differentiate it from the *hard skills* needed to work on machinery. Today, these skills (conflict resolution, communication, etc.) are rebranded as **power skills**.

Isn't it ironic? Don't ya think?

1960s Books

Fed up with the demands of unpaid labor, women wanted to make their mark on the workplace. Popular books include *The Feminine Mystique* by Betty Friedan—a major player in the **feminist** movement. The book encourages women to want more from life than to be "just housewives."

Another workplace book of this era, *Business Adventures* by John Brooks is a favorite of Warren Buffet and Bill Gates. It promotes mastering both the technical and human sides of business (Haden, 2019).

1970s

The **'70s** saw a shift in the traditional power structures and usher in a new landscape that included more **women and people of color**. And here's when **Gen X**ers are born—future grunge-y folks, created in the disco era. Fax machines and floppy disks are amongst the technology of the time.

In a continued evolution and progression of **safety** standards, the United States created the Occupational Health and Safety Administration (OSHA) in 1970.

1970s Books

The hippie movement seeps into the workplace. Leadership starts to get more introspective. The concept of **servant leadership**—a leadership philosophy in which the leader's goal is to serve—is popularized by Robert K. Greenleaf (Greenleaf, 2002). The premise is that a leader should share power and prioritize the well-being of people and communities. This era sees the philosophical tides shift away from producing to please those at the top and flips the script. T*ake that, Ayn Rand*!

Spiritual **books** like Paramhansa Yogananda's *Autobiography of a Yogi* inspire many in the hippie generation of the '60s and '70s who would eventually become business leaders in the '90s and 2000s. Even though it was originally published in the '40s, it became a must-read for spiritually-minded people in this era. In 1974, a young hippie named Steve Jobs traveled to India after reading the book as a teenager. He would, of course, become the co-founder and chairman/CEO of Apple. He re-read the book every year of his life. When he passed away, mourners at his memorial each received a copy of the book.

1970s Media

1976's *Network* shocked audiences with its portrayal of a fictionalized TV network looking to improve ratings and includes the famous "mad as hell" rant, which many employees could relate to then and now (Lumet, 1976).

1980s

Millennials were born and **Gen Xers** joined the workforce during the **yuppified "greed is good"** era. Ayn Rand's philosophy of selfishness and stepping on the little guy to get ahead came right back. After being introduced in academia several decades prior, the term **"corporate culture"** is collectively used and accepted in the business world. In 1984, Apple's Macintosh was launched.

Reaganomics was based on the trickle-down theory (money will trickle down if you spend it) and supply-side economics. This practice decreased taxes for corporations, which stimulated economic growth...for a while.

1980s Books

The 7 Habits of Highly Effective People by Stephen Covey was a major business book of the time (*The 7 Habits of Highly Effective People®*, n.d.). The habits include:

1. Be Proactive
2. Begin With the End in Mind
3. Put First Things First
4. Think Win-Win
5. Seek First to Understand, Then to Be Understood
6. Synergize
7. Sharpen the Saw

1980s Media

Movies like 1980's *9 to 5* showed the comedic side of workplace revenge fantasies as Dolly Parton, Lily Tomlin, and Jane Fonda used their zany antics to overcome their mean, egotistical, lying, sexist boss (Higgins, 1980). Oliver Stone's 1987 film *Wall Street* introduced Gordon Gekko as the embodiment of '80s greed in the immoral world of stockbrokers.

1990s

Ushering in a more **reflective and technologically focused** era in the '90s, this decade moved away from the 'profits above all else' mentality of the '80s.

The world welcomed **Gen Z** in the '90s. The birth of the **internet** revolutionized communication, which led to cell phones, email, and personal digital assistants (PDAs). People in the workplace began to notice the **inner work** needed for effective leadership in the workplace.

With that, the field of **executive coaching** began to grow. Executive coaching is defined as "a learning approach that creates self-awareness, helps drive transformational change, and provides critical challenge and support," according to the *Center for Creative Leadership*. In **1995**, the International Coach Federation (ICF) was founded to create a space for all coaches to support one another and help grow the profession.

1990s Books

Greed...humanity...ruthlessness...introspection. The push and pull of these values continues in this decade. Moving away from '80s profit above all else, books like *Emotional Intelligence* by Daniel Goleman focused on **mastering your own emotions and understanding the emotions of others**. It's remained a popular book and philosophy used in many organizations decades later.

The 48 Laws of Power by Robert Greene, on the other hand, shares lessons on how to gain power at all costs. The book shows how to manipulate your enemies, keep others dependent on you, and take credit for others' work! While some readers saw the book as a blueprint for power in the workplace, others criticized Greene for promoting manipulation and deception. It's been described as "amoral, cunning, ruthless, and instructive." Creepy but interesting!

On the other end of the spectrum is *The Power of Now*. Written in 1997, it's about encouraging self-reflection and being present. Philosophical gems from the book include: "Power over others is weakness disguised as strength. True power is **within**, and it is available to you now" (Tolle, 2004).

The workplace started to work its way up Maslow's hierarchy in the '90s, moving closer toward **self-actualization**, which is "the realization or fulfillment of one's talents and potentialities."

1990s Media

"I'm right on top of that, Rose!" In the **film** *Don't Tell Mom the Babysitter's Dead,* Sue Ellen's manager, Rose, coaches her to say this when she gives her tasks. She wants to hear that Sue Ellen is on top of things and will figure out what needs to be done. But silly Rose—she didn't know that she hired a teenager.

In a true "fake it 'til you make it" approach to the workplace of the early '90s, inexperienced teenager Sue Ellen pretends to be an accomplished fashion professional to earn money to support herself and her siblings while her mother is away for the summer (Herek, 1991).

Many of us have felt we had to be *"right on top of that, Rose"* and not permitted to ask for help. We are expected to just know. Perhaps this explains the "fake it 'til you make it (and feel tons of anxiety that you will be eventually discovered as a fraud)" **imposter syndrome** that many millennials suffer from! We are on top of it…but what is *it* really?! It depends on those around us and the organization. It will vary from role to role, based on people's interpretation of you and the role.

1992's *Glengarry Glen Ross* depicts a textbook toxic workplace where salesmen are bullied and berated by uber-successful trainer Alec Baldwin who screams at the men that they need "you know what" (rhymes with smalls) to be successful in sales. *Glengarry Glen Ross* shows how desperate salesmen try to conform to a toxic landscape to survive, whereas *Reality Bites* shows how the new generation resisted the path set before them by the previous generation (Foley, 1992) (Stiller, 1994).

These movies shaped my (somewhat twisted and mainly confused) view of the workplace as a youngster.

2000s

The focus on **collaboration and meaning** grew in the 2000s as the **Millennials** entered the workforce amid instability and constantly evolving rules for engagement in an era of shifting values and norms. Podcasts were born and virtual communication became popular.

This era also included the **dot-com bubble bursts** and **housing market crashes**. In this era, Skype, Facebook, Gmail, Google, Facebook, Twitter, and the iPhone were all born (Atlassian.com, 2020).

2000s Books

In the 2000s, many in the workplace started to recognize the importance of those **soft skills** mentioned earlier. In the book *The 5 Dysfunctions of a Team* by Patrick Lencioni, the author names the following **dysfunctions** (Lencioni, 2009):

1. Absence of trust
2. Fear of conflict
3. Lack of commitment
4. Avoidance of accountability
5. Inattention to team results

2000s Media

In 2006, *The Devil Wears Prada* depicted toxic work environments within the constraints of a romcom/dramedy. US Vogue editor Anna Wintour is widely believed to be the inspiration for archetypal scary boss Miranda Priestly who torments her assistant, Andy Sachs. In the film, serious Andy isn't even a fashion fan, but she takes the job to develop her "serious journalist" chops.

She ends up with a fabulous transformation (no glasses!) and a closet of luxury duds, before rejecting the material and isolating path to power that Miranda models for her (Frankel, 2006).

How many Andys are there in the workplace, doing something that does not resonate with their values or passion?

2000's *Boiler Room,* on the flip side, shows a male-dominated, egotistical, machiavellian culture of an immoral brokerage. The "bro" brokers pump themselves up by quoting angry, misogynistic lines from *Glengarry Glen Ross* for "funzies" and delight in taking money from those they manipulate and deceive (Younger, 2000).

The 2000s also gave us the TV show *The Office,* the mockumentary comedy centered around the Scranton branch of the Dunder Mifflin paper distribution company. Michael is the self-proclaimed "world's best boss," the painfully unaware leader. His insatiable need to be loved clouds every decision he makes, leading to a range of office-wide shenanigans (Gervais, 2005-2013).

Many of us could relate to the painfully awkward workplace realities and different personalities. Seeing arch-enemies Jim and Dwight eventually become best friends gave us hope that we could one day reconcile with our workplace nemesis.

2010s

This era saw a merging between professional and personal personalities rather than a separation from decades prior. The era focused on soft/power skills to transform workplaces through concepts like **self-awareness**, **vulnerability**, **wellness**, and **authenticity**. The technological advancements of this time included artificial intelligence, robotics, workplace productivity tools, and mobile apps (Atlassian.com, 2020).

For better or worse, social media became part of daily life for almost every adult during this time. It also ushered in a new creator economy, where people began to make very lucrative salaries through social media apps such as YouTube and TikTok. In 2019, **mental health** was called out as a worldwide problem by the World Health Organization with nearly 1 billion depressed people around the world. And that was pre-Covid (WHO, n.d.)!

Could the mental health crisis be correlated with the *"always on"* social media culture? Say or do the wrong thing on social media and your job could be on the line. Many employees find this out the hard way.

The **Alpha** generation was born in this era. If Gen Alpha listened to their early childhood entertainers like the cartoon Daniel Tiger —based on Mr. Rogers' teaching—they will be in good shape with strong emotional intelligence and communication skills when it's their turn to enter the workplace (Santomero, 2012 - Present) (Rogers, 1968-2001).

Children, I have faith in you!! You got this.

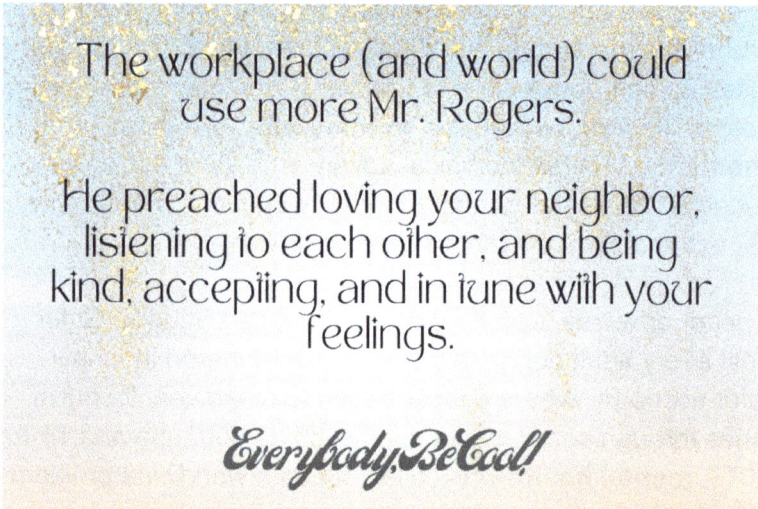

The workplace (and world) could use more Mr. Rogers.

He preached loving your neighbor, listening to each other, and being kind, accepting, and in tune with your feelings.

Everybody, Be Cool!

The decades-long effort for representation sees a major win as corporate **Diversity, Equity, and Inclusion (DEI)** initiatives become more popular in the workplace. Most companies with more job titles and leadership positions focused on DEI. DEI, depending on the organization, can also include terms such as **belonging (DEIB)** and **justice (DEIBJ).**

According to McKinsey, in 2020, businesses spent an estimated $7.5 billion on DEI-related efforts such as employee resource groups (ERGs). It's projected to more than double to **$15.4 billion by 2026**.

Power skills build upon soft skills to handle the mental agility needed to flex and adapt to a world that continues to change at a rapid pace (Bersin, 2019).

The prevalence of executive coaching and promoting coaching skills continues to rise and collide in **leadership development**. The virtual coaching company Better Up, formed in 2013, eventually becomes the largest mental health and coaching startup in the world.

2010s Books

Lean In tried to sell a controversial brand of feminism for working mothers. In the book, the author argued that women just needed to *lean in more* (get it?) to their careers, rather than avoid challenging roles at work when they become mothers. They just need to make their husbands do more stuff at home.

Why didn't ladies think of that before?!

We weren't leaning *enough*, ladies! No, the book didn't say that exactly. However, the book was criticized for its privilege and bias, oversimplifying the challenges and pressures faced by working mothers in a system not designed for them (Sandberg & Scovell, 2013) (Goldstein, 2018).

The Gifts of Imperfection by Brené Brown and her talk on shame became one of the most viewed TED talks. And the workplace went wild for Brown! A consistent leadership and workplace voice, Brown popularized the **workplace vulnerability** concept, which continues in the 2020s (Brown, 2012).

But, is workplace vulnerability really achievable—or even recommended—in practice? Is it just more privileged behavior disguised as openness? Vulnerability may be "cool" for leaders, but what about individual contributors, specialists, and doers of the workplace?

Can we declare that feelings are cool and share our innermost feelings during an all-hands meeting? *Cry* in the workplace?

While some may try to convince you that it's okay, this show of vulnerability is probably not as accepted in real life. Vulnerability is subjective depending on the whims of those around you and your position in the workplace.

Proceed with caution.

2010s Media

The film *The Big Short* centers around several stories that depict 2007's housing crisis. Three separate but parallel stories depict what led to the U.S. mortgage housing crisis of 2005, showing how greed and selfishness can impact the collective.

2010's *The Social Network* dramatized the origin story of future social media mogul Mark Zuckerberg, focusing on depositions from lawsuits centered around the founding of Facebook.

Both films depict environments where profit and power trumped human relationships and the good of humanity, denoting a swing to more of a "profits over people" approach (McKay, 2015) (Fincher, 2010).

Generations in the Workplace

Looking back, it's easy to spot the patterns of the generations entering the workplace and shaking things up. They demanded change based on their circumstances, whether **equality, safety, inclusion, or technology**.

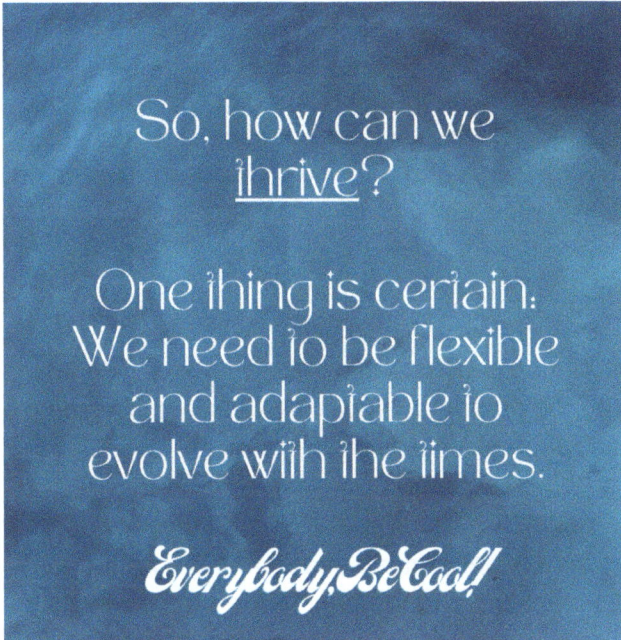

So, how can we thrive?

One thing is certain: We need to be flexible and adaptable to evolve with the times.

Everybody, Be Cool!

While there has been a strong focus on millennials in the workforce, they are no longer the newest kids on the block. Some millennials are nearing middle age, and many are in leadership positions (even CEOs). **By 2030, Gen Z will make up 30% of the workplace.** While Gen Z has gotten a bad rap for their perceived lack of work ethic, they are pushing the workplace to change and adapt rather than the other way around (The World Economic Forum, 2022).

Gen Z has a lot to say about what they are willing and not willing to tolerate in the workplace. This newest generation is living through a unique **period of transformation**. They are coming into the workplace, and they are demanding a psychologically safe, open, and caring environment that is going to help them grow.

The newest generation wants to see transformational change in the workplace and beyond. According to *World Economic Forum*, "Most of Gen Z are not opposed to a corporate job — they're just not as likely as other generations of employees to make compromises for a workplace that doesn't fit their values." Maybe they saw their parents struggle with unfulfilling careers and vowed to take a different route.

I say go for it, youngsters! Why not try at least?

Disruptive change is constant in the workplace. The last few years have blurred the standards and once definitive lives between personal and professional lives.

Workplace trends like The Great Resignation showed us that employees across generations are demanding more for themselves thanks to changes demanded by Millenials and Gen Z in particular.

According to BetterUp Labs, **74% of Millenials and Gen Z are ready to quit over a lack of development** (BetterUp, n.d.).

Some in **Gen Alpha** are already making money by sidestepping the workplace entirely as children (flashback to the early 1900s). However, this time, the focus is on the internet instead of factories.

This generation is getting in on the action with the creator economy.

As *Entrepreneur* points out, "Social media, streaming and video games opened a lane for younger kids to earn a living doing something that comes naturally, as they were the first generation born with iPhones and now ChatGPT. Experts say this can have benefits and consequences. Kids who work can get so caught up in their jobs that they miss out on essential childhood experiences they can never return to relive. This is a contributing factor to the growing loneliness epidemic among young people" (Grundhoefer, 2023).

Takeaways

In this chapter, we learned:

- **Remember, this push and pull between generations—the old and new way of doing things—is cyclical and normal.**
  - While the changes of the early 2020s may seem abnormal (or even apocalyptic), putting it in the context of the last several generations shows that it's quite normal. **Nothing stays the same.**

- **Be aware of the context in any group space you occupy.**
  - If you weren't taught it or were only taught a small sliver, **educate yourself**! Don't let someone shout *their truth* at you. Keep an open mind. Listen to diverse voices. **The sum of all those perspectives and opinions is a collective truth.**

- **In every decade, a revolution (or two) helped the workplace evolve to the next incarnation.**
  - So while the daily changes we are living through may feel uncomfortable, it's helpful to remember that times have always been in flux in one way or another.

- **Understand the patterns.**
  - When put into the context of decades and generations, extreme societal and workplace changes seem like part of a larger pattern, rather than a one-off anomaly.

Self-Reflection Activity

Instructions: *Sit and reflect. Comfy? Great. Now, travel back in time in your mind and think about when **you first joined the workforce**. Reflect on how far you've come and how much you've adapted since you first started. Which patterns or cycles do you recognize? Grab a pen or pencil and write down the answers.*

Optional Instructions: If you are just starting out, think about how you want things to be 10 to 20 years in the future.

Q: What is my ideal role and workplace? Picture it. Describe it. Manifest it.

_____

_____

_____

_____

_____

_____

_____

_____

_____

_____

_____

_____

_____

_____

_____

_____

_____

_____

Q: What was different when I first started my career?

_____
_____
_____
_____
_____
_____
_____
_____
_____
_____
_____
_____
_____
_____
_____
_____
_____
_____
_____
_____
_____
_____
_____
_____
_____

Q: What stayed the same since I started my career? *What's been the consistent thread?*

_____

_____

_____

_____

_____

_____

_____

_____

_____

_____

_____

_____

_____

_____

_____

_____

_____

_____

_____

_____

_____

_____

_____

_____

_____

_____

_____

Q: What has improved for me in my career?

Q: What's declined in my career?

_____

_____

_____

_____

_____

_____

_____

_____

_____

_____

_____

_____

_____

_____

_____

_____

_____

_____

_____

_____

_____

_____

_____

_____

_____

_____

_____

_____

_____

Q: What were the norms in the workplace when I first started working?

_____
_____
_____
_____
_____
_____
_____
_____
_____
_____
_____
_____
_____
_____
_____
_____
_____
_____
_____
_____
_____
_____
_____
_____
_____
_____
_____
_____
_____

Q: How have I changed since joining the workforce?

_____

_____

_____

_____

_____

_____

_____

_____

_____

_____

_____

_____

_____

_____

_____

_____

_____

_____

_____

_____

_____

_____

_____

_____

_____

_____

_____

_____

Q: Where do I see myself in 10 years? *Yes, it's that dreaded question, without the pressure of the annual review or anyone's judgment.*

Q: How can I get where I want to be in my career?

_____
_____
_____
_____
_____
_____
_____
_____
_____
_____
_____
_____
_____
_____
_____
_____
_____
_____
_____
_____
_____
_____
_____
_____
_____
_____
_____

Next Steps

Now that you've recognized the patterns and context of the present-day workplace—*commonly agreed-upon values, trends, influential media, books, and ideas*—this will help orient you in the present.

Be on the lookout for **more patterns** and emerging trends as you navigate your career. Identifying patterns will help prepare you for a new cycle to emerge. And it will help you make sense of your landscape.

Read on to discover the next lesson—**Journey into your awareness**.

Lesson #2: Journey into your awareness.

"Who am I?

Where am I going?"

Tony Soprano—a "strong" (often emotional, harsh, and reactive) leader in the HBO classic *The Sopranos*—once asked those same introspective questions after a near-death encounter with his uncle in the show's final season. I'm sure you've asked yourself similar questions (hopefully in different circumstances) in your workplace or life. If you haven't yet reflected on where you're going, there's still time!

The workplace can trigger existential questions, especially in performance and career development discussions. That begs the question... *What's your inner world like? How do you talk to yourself? What do you think about the things that happen in your life?*

The actual way that you think—**your inner monologue**—makes all the difference in your life satisfaction, resilience, relationships with yourself and others, and how you communicate your story.

Workplace culture varies from organization to organization, but no matter where you are or what you've been through, you can shape your narrative and **experience**. Here's a suggestion on how you can make the workplace better, one person at a time—starting with yourself. Work on developing your heart and mind.

Introspection as Personal/Professional Development

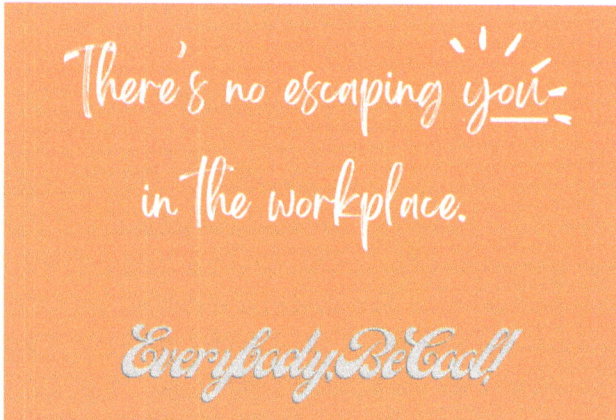

If you're selected as a leader in your organization, you may already have a personal/professional development roadmap. Coaching may be available for some executives and leaders in the workplace, but it depends on the organization's budget and priorities. However, everyone can benefit from the tools and benefits that coaching can give you.

Even the people who are not designated as leaders in their organization…yet.

Coaching can help you develop **self-awareness, higher levels of consciousness, active listening**, **problem-solving, conflict resolution,** and more good human stuff. This style of professional development is really personal development since it transcends the workplace and can make you a better person with better relationships. When you grow as a person, it also positively impacts your work as well.

Coaching is not only good for individuals and their personal development; it's good for business too. According to *BetterUp Labs*, companies with a robust **coaching culture** experience a performance boost of up to **24%** and reach **20%** more of their goals (BetterUp, n.d.).

Why wait for a leadership role to level up your awareness? The sooner that you start, the better. And the sooner you prime yourself for opportunities that come your way.

Be open to change, growth, and transformation.

One of the reasons I wrote this book is to address how we each have more power than we think. We aren't just victims of instability and crisis. Recall the lesson in the previous chapter—there's always chaos and change around us. When nothing feels stable and the old attempts at security such as **saving money and working hard** don't work like they used to, we can always go inwards and work on ourselves.

Having a clear direction and understanding of where you want to go in your career is always important. If you put too many expectations on an organization or a leader to lead you, you may find yourself far off course or not where you'd like to be. If you leave it up to an organization to determine what they want to do with you, you're making yourself vulnerable to their whims. Take control of your development. This way, it will be consistent even as you *(GASP)* change jobs.

If you are "going with the flow" or waiting for recognition, you may find, years or decades later, that the flow takes you someplace you don't want to go. **Take initiative and ownership of your journey.**

Aware vs. Unaware

"The primary cause of unhappiness is never the situation but thought about it. Be aware of the thoughts you are thinking. Separate them from the situation, which is always neutral. It is as it is." — **Eckhart Tolle** (Tolle, 2004)

People are either **aware** or **unaware**. What does that mean, exactly? The more **self-aware** each of us is, the better the workplace (and, by extension, our freakin' *world*) will be collectively. That's easier said than done, though. Self-discovery is not for wimps.

Do you consider yourself self-aware? Would others? If you're not sure, go ahead and ask a few close people in your life. (Don't yell at them if you don't like the answer. That might be a hint that you're not as self-aware as you think you are.)

According to *Psychology Today*, psychotherapy's aim is to **create holistic brain integration**, which in turn leads to healthy functioning (Narvaez, 2021). Therapist and trainer **Tiffany Totah**, who works for major companies in the Bay Area, shares, "Most people aren't healthy or **integrated** enough to address their issues. Or they don't have the energy or time to explore their inner worlds. We have to communicate within ourselves first before we communicate with others."

A *Harvard Business Review* study found that even though most people they spoke with believed they were self-aware, only **10% to 15%** of the people they studied fit the criteria of self-awareness (Eurich, 2018).

While many things are outside our control, many other things are within our control (even if it's just how our mind perceives our reality). We can create peace of mind at home and work (which is sometimes the same physical place). We have more access to tools and resources to support us in our pursuit of a happy life than ever before.

And there's much more of an open discussion around mental health than in years prior (both mental health in the workplace and general mental health). We have access to books, shows, podcasts, and all types of media that share best practices for mental health, self-care, and the pursuit of a happy life.

Aware individuals are strong enough in themselves to receive feedback and consider different perspectives. Unaware individuals are typically not receptive to feedback that challenges their own perspective. They usually get angry or defensive when presented perspectives that challenge their worldview.

While it's a lot to dive into your inner world, with these tools, you can navigate everything the world throws at you and thrive.

Which type of person are you? Which type of person do you want to be?

Accountability

Own what you put into the world.

That means acknowledging how you show up. And what does it mean to show up? Showing up means everything you bring with you: your unhealed trauma, your triggers, your **communication style**, and your ability to listen.

Are you lugging around the wounds from childhood that you never healed? Are you going to unknowingly act out those unhealed dynamics on those around you?

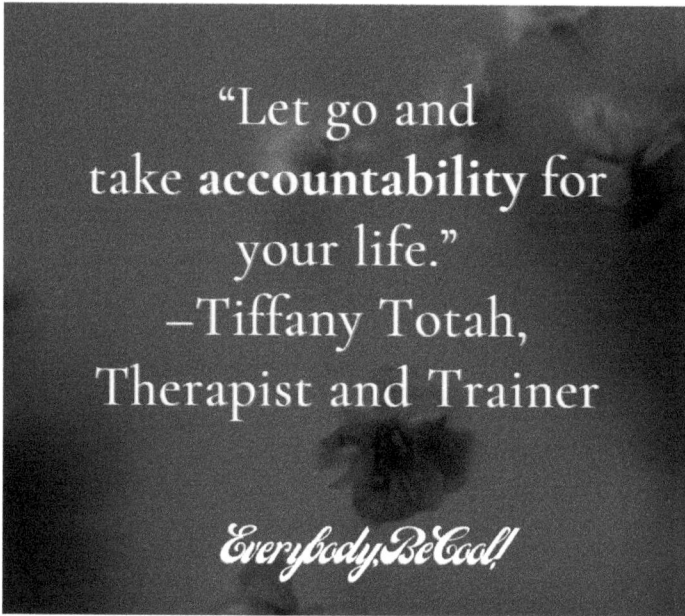

"Let go and take **accountability** for your life." –Tiffany Totah, Therapist and Trainer

Everybody Be Cool!

While acknowledging a variety of challenges and circumstances can impact our life experiences, it's also important to recognize the power individuals have to overcome challenges and create positive change within their own lives. Acknowledge **your part** in everything that led you to where you are.

What are the patterns in your life? As we learned in the previous chapter, understanding patterns is important in the larger context of a space you occupy. The same goes for your life in an individual context. Once you recognize these patterns, you can address them and the limiting beliefs around them. That's when the magic happens.

How ready are you to take responsibility?

Conscious people take responsibility for how their thoughts, beliefs, and emotions create their reality through their choices, decisions, and actions.

The media, events, and information you've consumed in your lifetime shape you, just like they shape each generation. Look for *your personal patterns* and see what can be reshaped.

Elevating Consciousness

"Strong convictions do not necessarily signal a powerful sense of self: very often quite the opposite. Intensely held beliefs may be no more than a person's unconscious effort to build a sense of self to fill what, underneath, is experienced as a vacuum."
— **Dr. Gabor Maté**, *When the Body Says No: The Cost of Hidden Stress* (Maté M.D., 2011)

To elevate your consciousness, you need to be open to growth. This includes knowing that you can't control the dynamics around you. No matter the state of the world or the workplace around us, the only thing you can control is **yourself**. Did you ever see that meme of the dog in the fire? The one where the dog stares blankly ahead and says, "This is FINE."

Is he numb? Or zen? It's open to interpretation.

Author and coach **Joelle Jackson** writes in her book *Unlock Your Conscious Leadership*, "Empowerment is an inside game." Jackson defines conscious leadership as an inclusive style of leadership that gets you to lead your **thoughts, beliefs, emotions, feelings, and actions from a *higher level of consciousness*** (Jackson, 2021).

And it's this definition of leadership that extends to everyone, as we all take leadership roles in different aspects of life (leadership of self, your family, etc).

Jackson writes, "Your inner genius is the voice of your wise self, as opposed to your ego or inner critic. It knows that you are already whole, perfect, and complete. It prompts you to make choices and decisions from that premise."

Do you listen to your **inner genius**? What do they tell you?

The goal of Jackson's conscious leadership philosophy is to realize the **four elements of your** *being*—your **mind, heart, body, and talent.** Once those four parts of yourself are realized, you can lead *yourself*, your family, and/or your team *consciously*.

Tapping into your consciousness is just one approach to creating a deeper relationship with yourself.

4 QUADRANTS OF BEING
JOELLE JACKSON

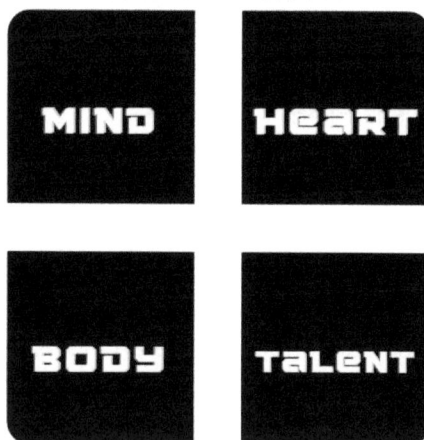

MIND	HEART
BODY	TALENT

Tuning In

It's also how *we perceive reality on an individual level* that has much more power than we realize. It's how we show up that impacts the collective. If our mind tells us **"you can't"** or "everything is awful," then we'll see more of our beliefs. The real test is centering ourselves and rejecting that reality, even (and especially) when faced with insurmountable challenges.

Do you feel in tune with your higher self? Try quieting everything down. **Grace Redman**, entrepreneur, success coach, podcast host, and author of *Can I Live?!* says, "We all have everything within us. The answers are within us. When I'm in a quiet place with myself, those answers ALWAYS come. Society has conditioned us to be distracted 24/7. This distracts us from communicating with our **higher self**. At the end of the day, the more that society is disconnected from itself, the less powerful we are as a whole."

Here's the secret to not getting caught up in whatever's happening: As the great teachers of meditation remind us, **anchor YOURSELF** in this exact moment in time to be fully present. RIGHT NOW.

Pretty simple, right?

Not really, I know.

But journeying inward doesn't have to be so complicated. CEO and Founder of Ascension Human Optimization and Performance **Arsalan Al Hashimi** advises how to get started on your inner journey. "Find something you enjoy and start easy. What do you gravitate towards? Is it: sleep, food, recovery, spirituality, books, or podcasts? That opens the door to see what you're interested in. The path guides you but **you** have to open the door!"

Can you open that door?

Start with what interests you and allow your curiosity to lead you.

Identity

"Much of what we call personality is not a fixed set of traits, only coping mechanisms a person acquired in childhood."
— **Dr. Gabor Maté**, *When the Body Says No* (Maté M.D., 2011)

When our jobs are our identities, layoffs can be a blow financially and even spiritually. It doesn't have to shake us at our cores. It's par for the course within a capitalistic system. There's what we do to pay our bills and who we are at a fundamental level. Those two things need to remain separate and with healthy boundaries. When those two things are linked, it's not setting us up for success or wellness.

Neha Mandhani, executive coach and leadership development consultant, shares "Your job is not your identity. You're more than your resume or your logo. Don't miss the important things in your life because you are replaceable at work. No boss gets to decide your worthiness. You're worthy because of **who you are**!"

This is especially true if you've ever had a manager who just didn't like you. Ever experience that? It's no fun.

I once had a manager who was fixated on my face. She would scrutinize my expression on Zoom calls and repeatedly admonish me for my "smile not matching my eyes." It got to the point where I didn't feel safe being on camera with her. Just the thought of communicating with her gave me panic attacks.
In retrospect, I gave her way too much control over my well-being, but workplace bullying is intense!

When I tried to go off-camera with her to lessen my anxiety, she would demand that I come on camera and show my face. When I shared feedback with her about this behavior (which she invited), she accused me of "not being happy" and not being a fit for the company. She had just joined the team as a leader and wanted to shake things up and show the team who was boss. She said others on the team agreed about the mismatch in my facial expression. Even knowing about the anxiety she was causing, she still demanded that I come on camera and show her my face.

Even though HR talked to her about it and she was put on an improvement plan to combat her obsession with my face (among other things), she couldn't let it go. She said she was making progress in her coaching, but she was also very angry about being "forced" into an improvement plan by HR. After trying to seek help and support from others in the company to no avail, I gathered my face and left the team and company after a decade there. The face-obsessed manager was let go a short while later...*shocker*!

The point is that if we base our **self-worth** on the wellness or awareness of those around us or even those who have power over our fates, that opens us up to depression and anxiety. We can't give so much power to others in the workplace that it impacts us so deeply (but it's challenging).

And on the flip side, people won't thrive if you pick on them and make them feel uncomfortable. Check yourself. *Are you the problem? Is your inability to communicate or navigate a challenging situation affecting other people negatively?* No one ever wants to consider that they might be the one contributing to an uncomfortable situation. I'm sure my former manager told herself a story about me and my face.

In this uncomfortable situation, I realized that just because I worked with an unwell person who had an issue with my face shouldn't shatter the image of myself. If someone doesn't like your face, that's THEIR problem!! Another company or client will. If a situation isn't feeling good and you've tried what you can and you've worked on yourself as much as you can, **find a situation** that will work better for your life.

YOLO: You only live once. Life's too short to be miserable in a workplace that isn't fitting with what you want.

Therapy

"Trauma is not what happens to you but what happens inside you." — Dr. Gabor Maté, *The Myth of Normal: Trauma, Illness and Healing in a Toxic Culture* (Maté & Maté, 2022)

Are you a person? If yes, you should probably go to therapy. If you're AI, you can skip it...*for now.*

Heck, even Tony Soprano went to therapy. Not sure if that unlocked a shift in his consciousness or just made him a more aware criminal...Nonetheless, at least go to therapy for long enough to develop awareness and tools. And even if you don't think you need it. Just go for shits and giggles. At the very least, you can prove how much you <u>didn't need</u> therapy.

But I (and many coaches, mental health professionals, and personal development experts) would argue that we could <u>all</u> use some help in that department. A dedicated resource to listen to your fears, frustrations, and challenges, with acceptance and solutions. If your workplace has a therapy benefit, such as an employee assistance program (EAP) to offset therapy costs, use it!

If not, therapy is a great investment to make in yourself and it will pay dividends immediately and later in life. Companies like Betterhelp or TalkSpace provide affordable, virtual therapy and certain health insurance providers also offset the cost of therapy. It may also be covered by your medical insurance. Look into it and explore any benefits you may not realize you have. Leverage your resources!

I lost my mom, Nahida, at an early age. She was a great, loving mom and a beautiful person all around. And her absence left a universe-sized hole in my heart. I was put in group therapy of sorts at my well-meaning public school for other students who experienced loss. I'm not sure who led the group (*gym teacher…counselor…lunch lady?*). That's the funny thing about depression—it can cloud your memory. That time is a bit of a blur, but it was comforting knowing that other kids could relate to the feelings of deep despair and grief I had while also navigating being cranky teens.

Therapy is a way to process life. All the weird things. It's a tool in your toolbelt for when things seem unbearable.

While the trauma of losing my mom is still something I still deal with 25 years later, therapy helped then and continues to help.

We all have **trauma**. That early experience with therapy gave me a foundation to understand "best practices" for processing complicated feelings. And to understand that this is a tool available to us. It's a benefit of living in our modern era. Grief shows up in the most unexpected places. It follows us around. Decades later. In our parenting. In our communication. In our relationships. *Unhealed trauma* affects everything. You can empower yourself by healing your trauma as best you can. We can heal generational trauma. And for some of us, it's a LOT. And not necessarily something we can or should discuss at work.

Coaching

Coaching is a great complement to therapy. Working with a coach can help you find the answers to challenges you encounter in the _present_ rather than looking back at what already happened in the past. A coach helps empower you to remove obstacles in your life and find answers for yourself.

We can't compartmentalize and leave our emotions at "home." Coaching is like opening a window, getting fresh air, and showing you a new perspective.

To be alive means to experience suffering. _Why not minimize the unnecessary suffering?_ Coaches help you connect with yourself and live your best life. It helps you set goals and keep you accountable, so you achieve your goals. A coach cheers for you and encourages you while providing practical tools to help you get to where you want to go. You can find coaches online—several are quoted in this book and provide virtual coaching.

Meditation

Most of our thoughts and actions are on autopilot. I know you're probably sick of hearing this but, meditating will help you navigate your inner journey. Meditation makes you get intentional, reduce the chatter in your head, and be present. It not only helps you individually, but it's also good for business! Meditation reduces stress, makes teamwork easier, and improves job satisfaction and engagement (Headspace, n.d.).

Spiritual Business Moment: Through Tolle's deeply philosophical approach, you are operating not just as your role or from your limited point of view, but from a point of view that acknowledges our oneness as **one human family**. The greatest illusion with labels and divisions and titles is that we are separate when we are all **part of the same being**. Remember, "they" is actually "we" on a grander scale.

Trippy, right?!

Is that philosophy possible in the workplace? Yes. Anything is possible. Why not aim for **love**?! If you think we could use more of it in life, start with one place you have control: **yourself**. The more you love yourself, the greater your capacity to love others. You never know what someone else is going through. Why not make someone else's day better instead of worse?

If coaching or therapy aren't options, there are always more **books** on the topics you can read to learn more about spirituality, introspection, and self-help. Be open and curious to a new way of processing life. It may help in ways you never imagined. Doesn't hurt to try, does it?

Connection

One way to show love is through kindness. Again, you never know what someone else is going through. Many of us are experts at faking being okay.

You can't be kumbaya with everyone but manifesting **love, peace, and connection** has more of an impact than we know. At least start with curiosity rather than judgment. Kindness rather than cruelty.

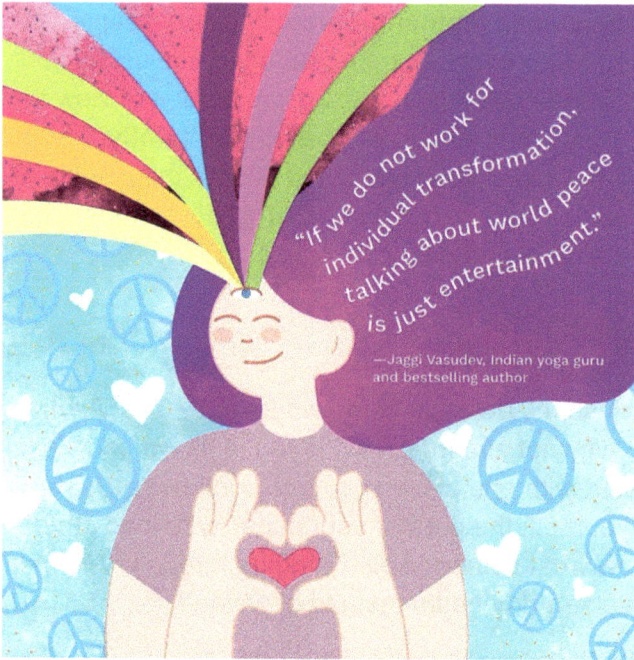

"If we do not work for individual transformation. talking about world peace is just entertainment."

—Jaggi Vasudev, Indian yoga guru and bestselling author

And we can apply that to the workplace and life in any of our interactions, as we'll explore more in the following chapters in conflict styles, communication, and navigating emotions. But it starts with us first and how we show up every day, in the spaces we occupy and in the roles we take on. If we're hurting, we need to be aware of how that hurt can manifest and affect others, which causes (you guessed it) more **pain**.

Even if we're hurting, we can choose not to hurt others. Lashing out at others and being reactive is not in the interest of our highest vibration. We WILL mess up, but we can do our best and take **accountability** when we inevitably falter.

It's like the patterns we observed in *Lesson 1*. Observe the patterns.

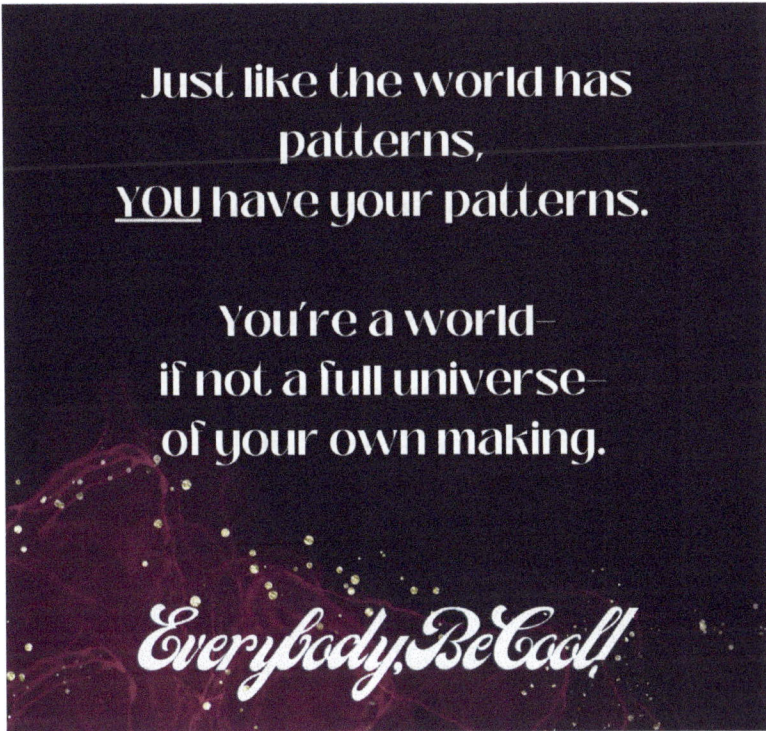

> # Just like the world has patterns,
> # <u>YOU</u> have your patterns.
>
> # You're a world–
> # if not a full universe–
> # of your own making.
>
> ## *Everybody, Be Cool!*

Together, humanity can **evolve our consciousness**—one person at a time. When we can evolve our consciousness, we minimize the awful things and *manifest* more wonderful things. It starts with each of us, so if you are even working on this, <u>you are doing your part</u>.

Takeaways

In this chapter, we learned:

- **Take a look at <u>yourself</u>.**
  - It's not easy to ask yourself these hard-hitting questions and face some tough truths. Being self-aware is not for the weak! But if we put our ego aside, we can see who we truly are and what makes us happy.

- **There's no escaping YOU in the workplace.**
  - Your mental health and self-awareness will impact your work and life. Society's collective beliefs and narratives may not always align with <u>your awareness</u> as you develop. Self-discovery is a lifelong endeavor. It's not a one-and-done. Learn and use all the tools available to you!

- **Go to therapy!**
  - Use your benefits if your workplace has an employee assistance program (EAP) that can offset therapy costs! And if you have to pay out of pocket, you can use virtual services. Explore your health insurance provider benefits.

- **Be open to change, growth, and transformation**.
  - In a poly-crisis world, we can't cling on to the "old way" of doing things. We have to adapt and adjust as new (and weird) events unfold.

Self-Reflection Activity

Instructions: *Sit and reflect. Reflect on how you show up at work and beyond. Get comfortable and find uninterrupted time and a quiet space. Really give yourself space and time to reflect deeply. Avoid multitasking.* Think about your awareness and inner-self.

Q: How would I describe my relationship to myself?

_____

_____

_____

_____

_____

_____

_____

_____

_____

_____

_____

_____

_____

_____

_____

_____

_____

_____

_____

_____

_____

Q: Am I self-aware? *What do I know about myself? What do others tell me about myself that I can't see?*

_____
_____
_____
_____
_____
_____
_____
_____
_____
_____
_____
_____
_____
_____
_____
_____
_____
_____
_____
_____
_____
_____
_____
_____
_____
_____
_____
_____
_____

Q: What experiences shaped my life or had the most impact on me?

_____

_____

_____

_____

_____

_____

_____

_____

_____

_____

_____

_____

_____

_____

_____

_____

_____

_____

_____

_____

_____

_____

_____

_____

_____

_____

Q: How does my unhealed trauma affect me?

How does it affect others around me?

_____

_____

_____

_____

_____

_____

_____

_____

_____

_____

_____

_____

_____

_____

_____

_____

_____

_____

_____

_____

_____

_____

_____

_____

_____

_____

_____

_____

Q: What would my life look like if I healed my trauma? *Picture an ideal scenario. Describe it.*

_____

_____

_____

_____

_____

_____

_____

_____

_____

_____

_____

_____

_____

_____

_____

_____

_____

_____

_____

_____

_____

_____

_____

_____

_____

_____

_____

_____

_____

_____

Next Steps

Extra Credit:

If you're not sure how others see you and you'd like to get more insight, **ask for feedback**!

To get effective feedback, identify the right people to ask—people you trust and respect. Prepare the questions beforehand. Determine if it will be in person, via Zoom, or via email/text/phone call. Take notes (if it's during a conversation). Thank the person for sharing. Then, reflect on their feedback.

Now that you've journeyed into your awareness and recognized how **trauma** impacts you, you can explore life tools such as **coaching** and **therapy.** Doing the tough work of introspection will make you more aware and give you a good idea of how you show up in the workplace. Be patient with yourself as you put in the work.

This foundation is necessary to understand how you work with others and help you elevate your consciousness.

Read on to discover the next lesson—**Improve your communication.**

Lesson #3: Improve your communication.

Every day, you can choose how you act, react, and communicate with others in every aspect of your life. Should you shout out your window at the person in front of you in the coffee shop drive-thru: *"Move, dumbass!?"* Or do you want to wait patiently for two seconds for the car in front of you to scoot up five feet?

Would you prefer to snap at your child or have patience and explain things calmly with kind words? After all, kids are sensitive and perceptive. They can sense even low-key stress and tension in their parents.

Seems like a no-brainer, but *stress, emotions, and trauma* can get in the way and cloud our choices. Improve communication and watch your personal life drastically improve. Do you want to go around with unchecked emotions and have outbursts toward those unfortunate enough to cross paths with you? Or do you want to contribute to a better day for those around you?

Going inward and developing **self-awareness** (as discussed in *Lesson #2—Journey into your awareness*) is the first step in improving **communication**. It's one of the most important skills you can master.

Think about it. Communication makes all the difference in all your relationships. That includes relationships with your *manager, colleagues, wife, husband, kids, friends, and neighbors.* **Everyone in your life.**

Power skills—also known as *soft skills*—are powerful for a reason. These skills encompass:

- Empathy
- Authenticity
- Active listening
- Curiosity
- Growth mindset
- Kindness
- Conflict resolution
- Emotional intelligence
- Giving and receiving feedback
- Managing challenging conversations
- Storytelling
- Effective decision-making
- Communication skills

*…All the **greatest hits of humanity**!*

You could and SHOULD be improving your communication skills throughout your career, wherever you land. But the job is never complete. This is a lifelong endeavor.

No one is a perfect communicator.

Not even master communicators like *Adam Grant*. I'm sure Mr. Grant and other incredible speakers aren't always poised and reasonable in every encounter they have in life. They too are human, get hangry, and let anger get the better of them.

The inner journey begins with **reflection**. Take a moment to reflect on your own communication style. Before you work on the outer communication, work on the *inner communication*.

Inner Communication

How can you expect to communicate effectively with others if you can't communicate with *yourself in a healthy way*? As discussed in *Lesson #2—Journey into your awareness*, having a strong connection with yourself and awareness of your inner-self is important for everything you do in life and work.

As we learned in the previous chapter, there's no escaping you, *so you might as well make friends with yourself, yeah?*

When I first started on my conscious coaching engagement with author and conscious coach **Joelle Jackson**, I had a **"woe is me"** narrative in my mind. When I thought about my career, my narrative was that I had been treated unfairly, overlooked, and undervalued. I'd dealt with egos, politics, power-hungry backstabbing, favoritism, biases…you name it! Colleagues and even managers unleashed their unhealed trauma and insecurities onto me.

One day in a coaching session, Joelle asked me, *"What if you flipped that narrative and changed the story you told yourself? How could you spin it another way?"*

So, I took a step back and thought about my experience in the workplace, starting out as a confused college graduate to the mom and professional I was at the moment. I opened a Microsoft Word doc and started getting creative, putting "fingers to keyboard." I reworded and rewrote this narrative to empower rather than victimize. I gave myself power by shifting the narrative into a growth and learning opportunity, i.e., *"Here's what I learned."* You can see a situation a certain way or *shift your thinking around it*. It's a subtle but powerful distinction.

In **Jackson**'s book, she writes, "You can **rewrite** how you remember certain events in your life when you feel victimized to empower yourself."

As someone who used to berate myself for not knowing things I had no way of knowing, I had NO IDEA how hard I was on myself until I started unpacking my stream-of-consciousness voice. That voice was pretty mean to me! It cursed me out regularly. I had no idea because it was so insidious. And it "should"-ed all over me: *"You should know this"* or *"you should do this."* And the irony was, I would turn around and advise friends to be kind to themselves while cussing myself out for the slightest perceived error or shortcoming. Not too cool, but it was so automatic and unconscious that I wasn't even aware until I stepped back and evaluated it. I didn't realize that this was my default, negative way to motivate myself.

I realized through therapy, meditation, and coaching, that I was operating from "fight-or-flight." Since I was in a workplace where I supported subject matter experts, I was telling myself that I didn't know things or topics that I should. Yet, there was no way I could know those things. I wasn't an engineer, so why would I know technical concepts? It was an unreasonable expectation. But I didn't even realize I was doing it at the time.

This default and unconscious approach and working with domineering personalities in a complicated workplace landscape affected my inner and outer communication. I was constantly walking on eggshells. Examining this helped me call out my unconscious behaviors and self-limiting beliefs. *How could I expect the workplace to value me when I was beating myself up?* I had to model what I wanted to see happen with my self-talk before I expected the outer conditions to change.

As **Elizabeth Leiba** tells us in her book *I'm Not Yelling: A Black Woman's Guide to Navigating the Workplace,* "How we speak to ourselves matters. What we say about ourselves matters. And I make a conscious effort to speak **to** myself and **about** myself with love" (Leiba, 2022).

Speak <u>**to and about**</u> yourself with <u>love</u>. Even—especially—if it feels. Force it if you have to. Give yourself credit. Talk to yourself the way you'd talk to a friend. Hype yourself up. If you won't do it, who will?!

Listening—both to yourself and others—is an act of love. Often, it's how we experience other people's love and self-love. And it's all too rare.

Listening

Have you ever felt ignored at any point? Ignored? Devalued?

An often-neglected yet integral piece of good communication is **listening**. Many of us don't feel listened to at some point in our lives—whether it was a distracted authority figure in childhood or as adults in the workplace. When someone does listen, it can feel like a pleasant surprise. Listening to others makes good communication...*who would have thought?!*

And no, not in the "We hear you" way that Cousin Greg from HBO's TV show *Succession* wanted to brand fictional media conglomerate ATN's ability to eavesdrop on its customers. There's hearing and then there's <u>listening</u>. You can hear someone, but not really listen to them. Hearing can be accidental, but listening is intentional.

"Walk down the street of any city, any afternoon, and look around you.

What you've got to remember is what you're looking at is also you.

Everyone you're looking at is also you.

You could be that person."

- James Baldwin,
Writer, Civil Rights Activist

Everybody, Be Cool!

(Baldwin, 1970)

If you want people to listen to you, listen to other people. And listen to yourself. Honor yourself. You're a person too!

If we want to see more kindness in the world, we can start with how we communicate with each other—with **kindness, curiosity, and respect**. If you are truly curious about another person and approach them with Baldwin's mindset, you'll be more apt to listen to them and connect. Rather than waiting for your turn to talk, true **empathy** helps you picture yourself in another's shoes. This is a technique that the world tells us we should embrace, although it's not always modeled, especially by those in power.

In busy cultures, taking time to connect is not always prioritized. We're chained to our calendars and inboxes and to-do lists. Our value is tied to our productivity. Think about your own life. Are you open when you're having conversations? Or are you waiting to get in your talking points?

Challenge yourself to engage people in conversation and get curious about their lives. Collectively, our social skills amount to a muscle that has experienced atrophy due to Covid.

Actually listening to another person is a demonstrable way to express **empathy**. According to *Merriam-Webster*, empathy is "the action of understanding, being aware of, being sensitive to, and vicariously experiencing the feelings, thoughts, and experience of another."

Empathy as a concept is discussed a lot in the workplace and written about extensively. We hear about it as often as we talk about *Q1 goals* and *ROI*, but embodying it is an entirely different experience. Many in the workplace have different definitions of empathy and different rules for who can be empathetic and in what way. *Is it sincere? Performative?* In the last several years, we've also seen empathy weaponized in the workplace, which **gaslights** employees while dismissing their actual needs.

There are also different types of empathy: cognitive, empathic, emotional, and so on.

One step beyond active listening is **empathic listening**, which is a "structured listening and questioning technique that allows you to develop and enhance relationships with a stronger understanding of what is being conveyed, both intellectually and emotionally." This focus helps you stay present in the moment rather than letting your brain wander off somewhere and return when the other person stops talking. (Mind Tools, n.d.)

Do you maintain eye contact with the person you are talking to? Do you zone out when someone is talking? Are you too distracted to listen?

Listen to the people in your life, workplace, and around the world. When we really listen to people, that's when true empathy can take place. When we listen, we empathize. It starts with *you*. How do you interact with people in seemingly unimportant encounters? Your neighbors, colleagues, friends, and community members.

How do you speak to a colleague in a meeting? How do you speak to a stranger on the internet? If you see something on the news you don't like—*oppression, hate, injustice*—you can start to **counteract it with how you act right at work and at home**.

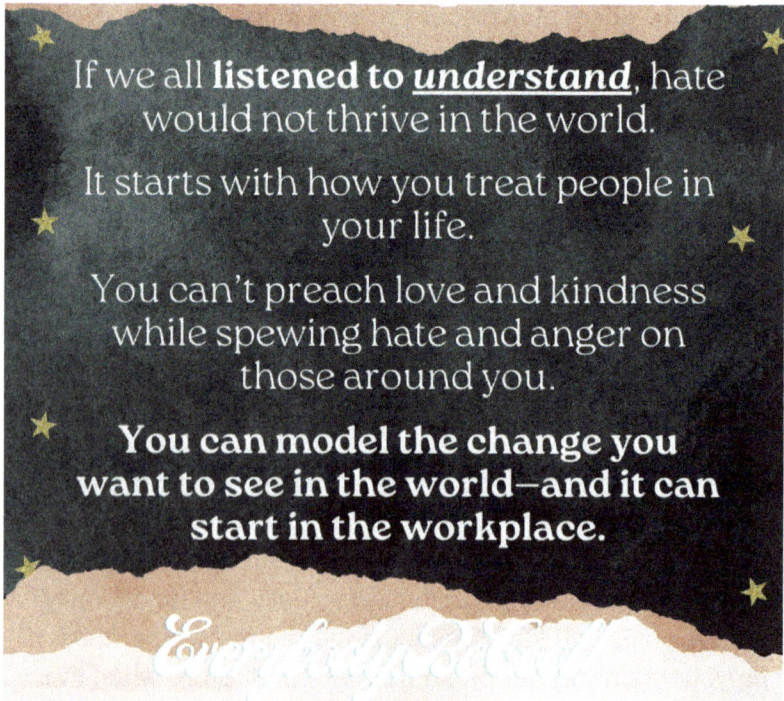

If we all **listened to _understand_**, hate would not thrive in the world.

It starts with how you treat people in your life.

You can't preach love and kindness while spewing hate and anger on those around you.

You can model the change you want to see in the world—and it can start in the workplace.

Communication & Culture

To cultivate a great culture at your workplace, you need to have a foundation of communication that everyone understands. It's the cornerstone of culture. Many types of communication—*meetings, presentations, informal interactions*—affect the collective workplace culture. It all adds up to each employee's **unique lived experience**.

Alethea O'Dell, chief marketing officer, brand strategist, and my former manager says, "How you experience culture is filtered through **how you see life**. There can be tension inside of that. Self-awareness, self-reflection, and curiosity for other people's perspectives contribute to a great culture."

Neha Mandhani—executive coach and leadership development consultant—asks, "What behaviors does your organization tolerate? Do you have a bully on your team but brush it off because they are good at their job?"

Your company can claim to be an empathetic place that accepts and respects all people, but its **actions** **speak to its values—not just words on its website**.

Even if your company may not have a communication standard, you can still direct your own communication growth. Leadership & development coach **Ellen Gillis** warns, "Keeping **toxic people** in your organization affects your culture's power dynamic and how people communicate and resolve conflicts. This behavior can trigger doubt in others in your organization. It sends the message that someone has to be *aggressive and manipulative* to be successful at the company. That person is causing toxicity and causing others to mimic."

A company-wide communication philosophy ensures a workplace culture can grow and scale. Organizations need a common language. Adopting a common language has to be a **change management effort** across the organization. At the least, employees need access to resources that help them have important and difficult conversations.

How does your workplace address communication? Do they follow a communication philosophy? *Crucial Conversations? Radical Candor?* Whatever it is, learn it, and apply it. Keep practicing. Find an accountability partner to help you reach your goals (i.e., speak more directly, communicate more empathetically, etc.).

Tiffany Totah encourages companies to: "Focus on communication, neutrality, and tools to manage employees' emotions. Provide tools to get people to go within so you can all speak the same language. Colleagues with tools and neutrality can navigate any situation. Communication begins within one's self first."

She asks "Can we cut the BS and say what we mean and mean what we say?"

Amen.

With kindness and respect, of course. But clear is kind. Be clear about what you are trying to communicate, and listen to the person you're talking to. How we choose to communicate sets the tone for your life. So, why not look for ways to improve your approach? Communication help is available in many forms.

Get Help

Whatever your workplace offers for communication resources or training, take the **resources** and run with it! **Never say no to more communication training.**

Ellen Gills says, "The biggest challenge that comes up in any coaching or leadership training is the *art of communicating*, whether that's listening or giving and receiving feedback. It always comes back to good or bad communication skills."

Know that you won't know everything. And to be good at communication, you will always be learning. Most of our employee experience boils down to how colleagues communicate with others in the workplace. *Is the communication respectful? Can employees resolve inevitable challenges effectively?*

How you express yourself and relate to others makes all the difference. When you approach communication consciously and get past reactivity, you and the other person can experience a **win-win**. How you communicate also affects the conflicts in your life, which we'll cover in **Lesson #4 - Understand your conflict style**.

After all, with no communication, there can be *no conflict resolution*.

If you want to **upskill your communication**, you have lots of options, such as (but not limited to):

- Virtual courses
    - Udemy, Coursera, Masterclass, LinkedIn Learning, etc.
- In-person training
- *Harvard Business Review* articles
- Books
- Apps
    - Orai, Speako, Likeso
- Podcasts
- Coaching
- Communication assessments
- Accountability partners

As *The Office*'s Michael Scott once hatefully said to his workplace nemesis Toby, "Why are you the way you are?"

Think about why *you* are the way you are. Maybe with a little more compassion than Michael had for Toby.

What is limiting you in getting you what you want in life? Are you avoiding talking about something? Do you get angry or frustrated when trying to communicate your needs? Do you ignore an issue until it explodes in a fit of rage? One communication resource mentioned is **work style assessments**. They can help determine why you are the way you are.

For example, **DisC assessments** are one way you can measure interpersonal behavior. You answer some questions and you will get a report that shows what motivates you and how you operate. It classifies how you interact in terms of four personality styles: **Drive (D), Influence (I), Support (S), and Clarity (C)**. It plots how strong your motivators are in each style (DiSC, n.d.).

Another tool is the Predictive Index's PI Behavioral Assessment, which analyzes your natural behavioral drives, needs, strengths, common traps, and how to work well with other profiles. After taking a quick quiz, you receive a report about yourself that explains your profile. There are 17 reference profiles such as *adaptor, collaborator, captain, etc.* The styles are built on four factors: **dominance**, **extraversion**, **patience**, and **formality** (The Predictive Index, n.d.).

Another assessment is **Enneagram.** It helps you understand which personality type you are, offering nine types, such as T*he Reformer, Helper, Peacemaker* (me!), etc. (Enneagram, n.d.).

Having that information helps you understand your communication style (and your colleagues). It's like having your own **User Manual** for yourself. It's not written in stone but it gives you an idea of how you operate. It's great to return to when you're starting a new project, assembling a new team, or gearing up for an important conversation. You can return to the report and read it weekly/monthly to see what your baseline is and how you are progressing towards any goals you've set.

And just like your inner discovery, this is also a lifelong journey.

Always be open to **learning, unlearning, evolving, and growing**.

As mentioned in the previous chapter, **coaching** is another powerful tool at your disposal (either on your own or through a company benefit if available). It helps you with your inner journey and your communication skills.

A coach is someone who is invested in your success. They will help keep you accountable to the goals you've set and the direction you want your life to take. Think of them as your own personal cheerleader, cheering you on and giving you tools to get where you want to be. They will check in with you if you tell them that you are yelling *"move, dumbass"* at people.

Coaches will dig in and help you understand why you are lashing out and what you can do to improve your communication and life.

The more self-aware you are, the better you communicate and behave, and the better the world will be.

Takeaways

In this chapter, we learned:

- **Effective communication is one of the most important things in life.**
    - It's the most important skill you can learn. Be open to a lifelong journey of improving your communication. No one is a perfect communicator.

- **Practice active and empathic listening.**
    - Picture yourself in other people's shoes. Listen to understand rather than for your chance to interject.

- **Take any communication resource that you have access to and run with it!**
    - Improving your communication is an instant life upgrade.

    - If your organization doesn't offer any resources, you can access podcasts, LinkedIn Learning courses, articles, books, or apps.

    - You can also seek coaching on your own or through your company if they offer it.

Self-Reflection Activity

Instructions: *Sit and reflect. Reflect on how you show up at work and beyond. Get comfortable and find uninterrupted time and a quiet space. Really give yourself space and time to reflect deeply.* Think about your communication style.

Q: How would I describe my communication style?

_____

_____

_____

_____

_____

_____

_____

_____

_____

_____

_____

_____

_____

_____

_____

_____

_____

_____

_____

_____

_____

_____

_____

Q: What has been a communication challenge for me in my life?

_____

_____

_____

_____

_____

_____

_____

_____

_____

_____

_____

_____

_____

_____

_____

_____

_____

_____

_____

_____

_____

_____

_____

_____

_____

_____

_____

Q: How would I rate my active listening ability on a scale from 1 to 10? *Why?*

Q: How can I improve my communication style?

_____

_____

_____

_____

_____

_____

_____

_____

_____

_____

_____

_____

_____

_____

_____

_____

_____

_____

_____

_____

_____

_____

Next Steps

Extra credit:

1. **More reading!** Read books like *Crucial Conversations* and/or *Radical Candor* to kick up your communication style several notches. Find an accountability partner who reads the book with you and helps hold you accountable for implementing the techniques.

2. Reach out to people you trust in your life and ask for their feedback about your communication style (if you're brave). *Where are the gaps? What is the difference between your perception and theirs?*

3. Start a **library of free resources** at your organization if it doesn't exist.

Once you've learned about communication and ways to improve it, you'll have a great foundation to handle anything that comes your way in the workplace.

Read on to discover the next lesson—**Understand your conflict style**.

Lesson 4: Understand your conflict style.

As humans, we can't hide our **emotions** very well.

Even if we push emotions down, they somehow pop up somewhere else. Whereas in generations prior, there was more of a distinction between your work and personal life, as shown in *Lesson 1—Be aware of your surroundings*, those lines are now blurred.

Encouraging employees to be their "authentic selves" (and not separating the employee from the person) means dealing with <u>real human emotions</u>. **Conflict** is inevitable—*sorry, people pleasers*. How we manage and regulate our **emotions** makes all the difference in our ability to resolve conflict. The stakes could not be higher. How you resolve conflict directly impacts your life satisfaction.

Spiritual Business Moment: How we handle conflict can mean the difference between **heaven and hell**. Literally. The choice is ours. **The workplace is just one space** to practice this invaluable skill. On a *macro level*, managing conflict can make or break our society. Imagine if all the leaders in the world were in touch with their feelings, traumas, and communication styles. What a difference that would make in the world! As I write this in late 2023 and early 2024, the world seems hellbent on repeating the horrors of the past. Violence against children. Violence against families. Violence against civilians. Forced displacement. Starving populations as collective punishment. Destruction of the earth. Destruction of an entire group of people while it's live-streamed to the rest of the world. Aren't we supposed to be smarter than that? More "civilized?"

You can't carpet-bomb your way to peace and stability. Full stop. *"But, but, but"*....**No but.** Period. Exclamation point!

Disclaimer: If you need to argue with this point, please re-read *Lesson 2—Journey into your awareness*. Do some soul-searching. Meditate on love, equality, perspective, and existence until you can come back with **empathy for humanity**.

Picture yourself in the other person's shoes. *What's it like to be them? Can you consider life from their point of view? Can you find similarities?*

Examine the conditioning that may have made you immune to the suffering of a particular type of people.

Consider if you want to uphold and defend oppressive systems that benefit you but make other human beings suffer. Read books written by people you've "othered." You'll need much more inner work if you see another human as "less than" or if your empathy is selective. That's a spiritual issue. Sending you love and light.

If this *doesn't* apply to you, please continue reading.

What does this have to do with the workplace, you ask? **The same global conflict resolution principles are true in your life.** On a *micro level*, how you handle conflict affects your relationships with friends, colleagues, and family.

You can't emotionally carpet-bomb your way into a peaceful or happy life. While you may have little control over the geopolitical landscape, you can avoid **wars, struggles, and power plays** in your personal realm.

The outdated, selfish "dog-eat-dog" style is not sustainable. **We know better and can do better.**

And it starts with each of us as individuals.

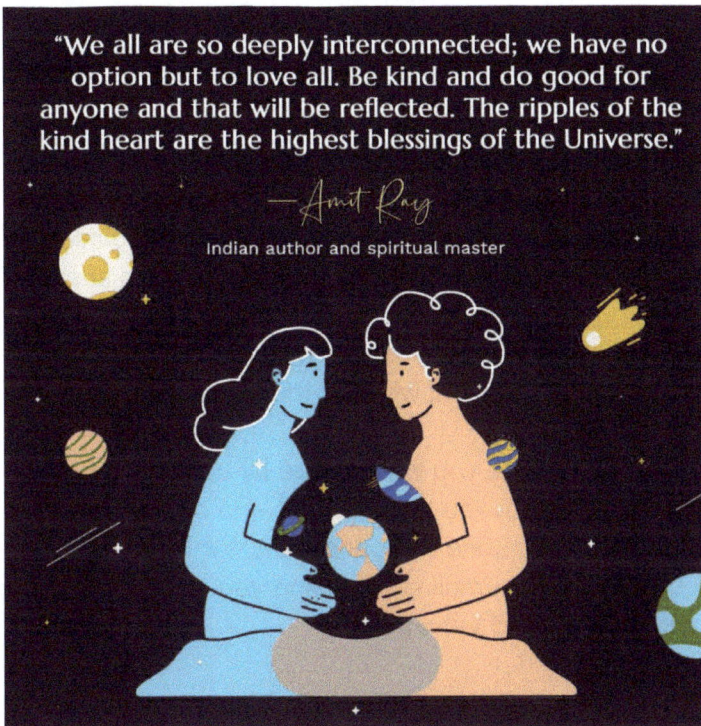

"We all are so deeply interconnected; we have no option but to love all. Be kind and do good for anyone and that will be reflected. The ripples of the kind heart are the highest blessings of the Universe."

—Amit Ray

Indian author and spiritual master

You can manifest *peace, love, and light* through proven **conflict resolution** strategies—and get what you want.

How you address conflict impacts the collective since we all are interconnected.

> "The tiny flame that lights up the human heart is like a blazing torch that comes down from heaven to light up the paths of mankind.
>
> 🔥
>
> For in *one soul* are contained the hopes and feelings of **all Mankind**."
>
> ❤️‍🔥
>
> —*Khalil Gibran, Poet and Philosopher*
>
> *Everybody Be Cool!*

Spiritual Business Moment: Remember that we are all part of a greater whole and we affect each other more than we realize. **Eddy Khawaja**, spiritual teacher and chief security officer for an international aid organization in the Western Sahara shares, "We are all one, <u>not separate</u> as we've been led to believe. The separateness is an illusion. We are waves in the same ocean. We're all part of one nation, which is the planet."

You can be the change you want to see by uplifting <u>yourself</u>. When you hurt others, you hurt yourself—no matter how much you've "othered" someone as your enemy. While you can't always control conflicts and turmoil surrounding you, you can **level up your own energy and vibration**.

The critical difference is your *emotions*. Your emotions impact your reactions, which cause a ripple effect across the universe. How you handle conflict dictates how the ripples affect others and, ultimately, <u>you</u>.

Conflict resolution skills can be your bridge across different realities. As you learned in the previous lesson, *words are your friends.*

Use your words carefully and strategically for outcomes that enrich your life. Realize the power in the energy you bring and the words you choose to connect (or disconnect) from another human being. Like its related concept—**communication**—conflict resolution may be one of the most challenging skills on earth to master, but it is possible.

You must understand the different conflict styles to improve your conflict resolution skills.

How do you navigate the waters when an issue arises between you and another person?

Conflict Styles

"Education is the ability to listen to almost anything without losing your temper or your self-confidence." — **Robert Frost**

The personal development field has become much more reflective. The most effective personal and leadership development programs encourage **self-awareness and introspection**. It can't be true that you're fine and perfect, but everyone else is the "problem." We all co-create our realities together. Acknowledging your part in things is key. You might be activating someone else's trauma without even knowing it! Maybe you remind them of their abusive mom or neglectful dad. This is why realizing how your worldview or trauma impacts your interactions with others is important.

How you manage your triggers and find common ground with someone you dislike or disagree with speaks volumes about your **emotional maturity**. It requires an exceeding amount of **self-control** and **self-awareness**. You'll either learn to deal with conflict or let your fear hold you back—*your choice.*

Fear tells you not to try. Another way it shows up is by telling you to ignore your feelings to make others happy. Take it from me—a reforming people pleaser. We people pleasers tend to avoid conflict by doing or saying whatever it takes to make everyone happy! That's not a healthy way to address conflict because it abandons your needs. This style puts everyone else's needs above yours, leading to resentment, frustration, and feeling unheard/unseen.

In the *Crucial Conversations* style of **conflict resolution,** based on the best-selling book of the same name by Patterson, Grenny, McMillan, and Switzler, for example, people often choose **silence or violence** when they start to feel psychologically unsafe in a conversation.

"Silence" refers to **masking, avoiding, and withdrawing from conflict.** People in the silent type will do anything not to fight. "Violence" refers to *controlling, labeling, and attacking when faced with conflict.* The violence style doesn't refer to actual violence but involves giving in to emotions like anger and fear. So, on one end of the spectrum of conflict styles, you feel fear or discomfort that makes you retreat from conflict; on the other end, you get angry, defensive, and confrontational.

Engaging in either of these styles will not resolve conflict. These techniques only make challenges grow into full-blown dramas (Grenny et al., 2021).

Let's explore an example of conflict resolution styles. Upset about a business deal gone wrong, Christopher (or *Christophuh* as his late fiancé used to call him) pushes his colleague Paulie's nephew out a window. Enraged, Paulie drives on Chris' lawn in angry circles, ruining the pristine yard while Chris' wife looks on in shock and terror from her window. Afterward, Paulie and Chris briefly reconcile. Eventually, Chris finds himself in another conflict with his leader, Tony, that results in his termination.

This, of course, is an example from HBO's '90s-2000s classic tv show *The Sopranos* (Chase, 1999-2007).

What is the moral of the story? ***Don't be Christophuh!*** This example of conflict resolution style is extreme, but it shows how emotions can cloud interactions, causing one-upping and vengeful behavior.

Robert Jackson, *Crucial Conversations* facilitator, talent advisor, and my former manager says, "It starts with the self. That's step one. What are YOU going to do differently? If we can start with ourselves first at ALL levels, seek perspective, and create psychological safety, it goes a long way in an organization."

The *Crucial Conversations* method shares techniques that help conversations avoid the "silence or violence" route and ensure that both voices and needs are heard and addressed. One of the techniques is to **seek a mutual purpose**.

Seeking a mutual purpose helps two parties in a conversation create a **win-win**. It also helps people avoid getting emotional, which derails essential discussions. If both parties can agree on and center a mutual purpose, it makes it less of a push and pull. It invites people to co-create collaborations that work for both parties. It's less about "you did this to me" and more about *"let's figure out how to accomplish this goal that benefits us both."*

When you point one finger at someone, three more are pointing back at you, as the saying goes. Take a pause and assess the situation. *Is it you?* Be strategic and make sure you aren't lashing out. This strategy will ultimately help you (ideally, the other party). There is power in the pause.

If Tony Soprano and the gang were more in touch with their feelings and engaged in *journaling, meditation, communication training, and other reflective activities*, they could have handled this disagreement differently. Tools that help with conflict resolution promote **emotional intelligence, managing the ego, neutrality, curiosity,** and **mindfulness**.

Emotional Intelligence

Ever work with someone who got on your nerves? Or could you tell that someone didn't like you?

It's okay. Being liked isn't guaranteed in the workplace, but <u>respect</u> should be. You won't like everyone at work. And not everyone will like you! Pobody's nerfect.

Christina Dyer says, "Daniel Goleman's work on emotional intelligence is a huge trend in corporations. Everyone wants emotional intelligence training. The first component is always **self-awareness**. The second is **self-mastery**. How do you change your behavior now that you know how you're behaving? How do you not get triggered? The third is **other awareness**. Now that you know and master yourself, how do you manage what others do around you? The fourth is **bringing it all home**, allowing you to join everyone and see the self-awareness and other awareness, and moving forward to set goals. Many leaders will say everyone needs to get on board with this model, but *they're* the ones who make the change."

The more we develop **emotional intelligence**, the more we understand ourselves and others. There needs to be comfort and understanding within yourself first. If you know yourself more, you can feel more comfortable putting yourself in others' shoes. Next, you have to get curious about other people. Realize that you can't take everything personally. How someone treats you says more about them than you.

Ego

"You must practice seeing yourself with a little distance, cultivating the ability to get out of your own head. Detachment is a sort of natural ego antidote. It's easy to be emotionally invested and infatuated with your own work. Any and every narcissist can do that. What is rare is not raw talent, skill, or even confidence, but humility, diligence, and self-awareness." — **Ryan Holiday**, *Ego is the Enemy*

Ego shows up often in the workplace. After all, people with big egos were positively rewarded in the workplace of the past (and today). While some people rely on bravado, self-promotion, and ingratiating themselves with decision-makers to get ahead at work, there are also those at the opposite end of the spectrum. Many employees put their heads down and perform, hoping that somebody will miraculously recognize their work. This can create feelings of not being seen or valued. Too little or too much ego can be problematic. It's about finding the right balance for you and your life. It can get activated more when we are **afraid**.

Neha Mandhani says, "Fear can be a useful guidepost and signal that points us to deeper insights about ourselves and what matters to us. It can also keep us safe. It can also hinder us. It's where our insecurities can come up. Our culture often uses fear as a bad word, but in reality, our fear can also serve us in a healthy way. It can inspire us to move forward and create and make decisions that align with our values. It's about time we learn to befriend our fear and work alongside it."

The ego can be a big issue in conflict resolution. When confronted with a high-stakes conversation, the ego may say things to you such as *"How dare they speak to me like that?"*

When your pride feels injured in a conflict, keeping the conflict healthy is hard. **Curiosity, neutrality, engaging the brain strategically, and mindfulness** are all tools in your toolbelt to resolve conflict. Use them!

Curiosity, Neutrality & Your Brain

Meet your **"lizard brain."** It's also known as your reptilian brain or amygdala. Our basic functioning neural system includes the brain stem, cerebellum, and basal ganglia. Your lizard brain is responsible for simple survival urges like feeding and defense. It's responsible for behaviors involved in aggression, dominance, territoriality, and ritual displays (AMNH, n.d.). It's also responsible for patterns and procedural memories (Budson, 2017).

Pattern recognition and procedure automation are important, but they also haven't had time to adapt to the workplace. Your brain is firing as if there's a literal physical threat when it's really just your colleague from Accounting being passive-aggressive.

The lizard brain kicks in when you allow your emotions to take over on autopilot. If you're angry and making decisions, you're making decisions from the older, less developed part of your brain. It's an involuntary response, but through changing your habits and reactions, you can change how your brain is wired (over time). You have to take the wheel. It's challenging, but possible!

When you see an image of someone you view as "other," your amygdala responds with **fear or readiness to fight or flee**—also known as **silence or violence**. It's up to us to manage it so that our frontal cortex can kick in, turn off the amygdala, and remind us to do better. Ideally, you will engage the **prefrontal cortex** to make your best decisions. (Morse, 2006) The prefrontal cortex shifts gears and gets you away from unconscious reactions. When you control your emotions and avoid going into "lizard mode," you can react more effectively, using the skills and strategies you've developed. It helps you envision the long-term perspective in evaluating risks and rewards. It's a process and a discipline, but if you can hang in there, you will reap the benefits of a more developed decision-making system.

Curiosity is a way to engage without getting emotional. Taking time to check your emotions helps determine which part of the brain you engage. Being intentional about your feelings will help you self-regulate. Notice the feelings that arise when you are triggered. *Do you feel your heart rate rising? What is changing in your body?*

Accepting yourself will go a long way. Make space for your emotions and thoughts. Spiritual teacher and yogi, **Maria Khawaja** says, "Think of your emotions as **clouds in the sky**. Observe them. Watch them come and go. Don't judge them."

You can be honest with yourself and admit even when you have "bad" feelings like jealousy or shame. Thoughts and feelings are okay! Feel them. "Right now, I am *feeling* <fill in the blank>," rather than "I *am* <fill in the blank>." Note the distinction between <u>feeling</u> and <u>being</u>. Words are powerful.

Acknowledge your feelings. And let them go. If you try to suppress or judge yourself or pretend the feelings aren't there, that's where the weird stuff happens.

Be kind to yourself. Think of yourself as a friend and don't be so hard on yourself. Crap happens. It crappens, if you will.

Neutrality and detachment can help you control your emotions to engage the prefrontal cortex. Adopt the persona of a social anthropologist by giving yourself some emotional distance and being mindful of your reaction.

Rather than take offense to someone, step back and get curious. If you can get past your ego and get curious, that's where the magic starts. Without curiosity, blind spots remain.

What is this other person trying to communicate? What is their perspective? What would a win-win look like for you both?

"The most powerful person is the <u>NEUTRAL</u> person!

If you get triggered, step back and come back in. We all want validation and to feel good.

Do you need it? Are you searching for it?

—**Grace Redman**, entrepreneur, success coach, podcast host, and author of *Can I Live?!*

Everybody Be Cool!

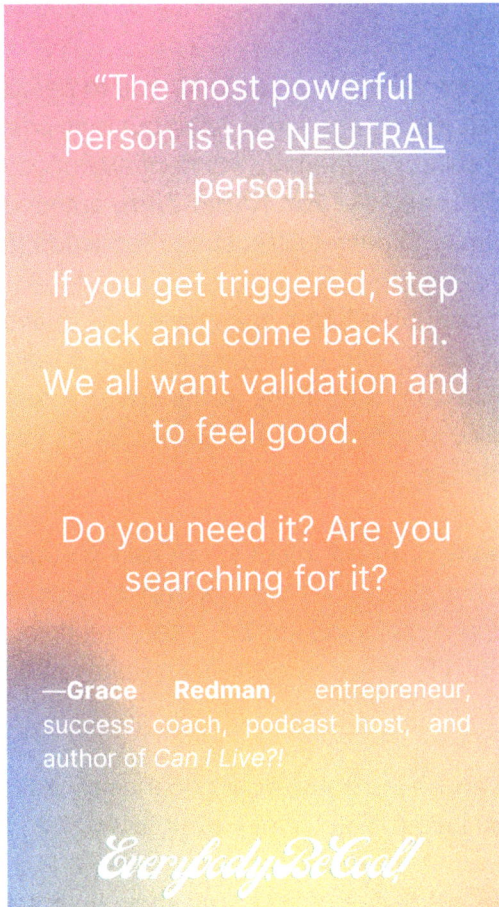

Grace's advice?

"The most important thing to cultivate is confidence in <u>yourself</u>. The more you overcome, the more experiences you have, the more confident you become. Find your **inner coach** and access them often. And if you need more support, reach out to a friend or watch YouTube videos on self-development. If it's accessible, invest in hiring a coach to help you."

Get Mindful

"The core invitation of mindfulness is for you to befriend yourself. That means recognizing and inhabiting your own intrinsic wholeness and beauty in the only moment any of us ever has—namely this one." -— **Jon Kabat-Zinn**, author, professor, and founder of mindfulness-based stress reduction (MBSR)

You've learned about the lizard brain (and how to avoid letting it take over), now you'll need to learn how to tame the monkey mind. Is it a coincidence that both of the terms are animal-themed? No, it's not. Our ability to reason is what separates us from our furry or cold-blooded friends.

In **yoga**, the **monkey mind** refers to our racing stream of consciousness (Hughes, 2017). According to Buddhist philosophy, the monkey mind is our uncontrolled, often negative, mental chatter (Raab, 2017). You can calm the monkey mind through **mindfulness**.

Mindful people share the natural gift of curiosity, which is intuitive to children. Kids love to ask: *"Why? Why? Why?"*

Mindful people are aware of how they show up in the universe, and at the same time, they are aware that everyone else around them is a complex human being (just like them). They are curious about others' lived experiences, not just their own. They know we all just want to feel accepted and like we matter.

Being mindful in the workplace also means being aware of your team and everyone you interact with. That includes acknowledging your teammates' perspectives to co-create a conscious, psychologically safe environment.

It all comes down to how you engage your brain—your most important resource!

Calm your monkey mind with **mindful techniques** *that include:*

- **Be present!**

    - *What does that even mean, right?* Believe me, I get it.

    - Your monkey mind is activated when it's ruminating about the <u>past</u> or stressing out about the <u>future</u>.

    - Stay in the moment to avoid the depression or anxiety that comes from looking backward or forward. Just be. Focus on the exact moment you're in—not five minutes ago, tomorrow, or next week.

    - Try the 5-4-3-2-1 technique to help you stay present. (Smith, 2018)

- **Meditate!**

    - Meditation is another great way for you to be present. As the great spiritual teacher **Ram Dass** says, "All you have to do for the next three minutes is attend to your abdomen, that's all you've got to do. You don't have to listen to the sounds outside, you don't have to think about your body, you don't have to do anything. Just put it all in neutral."

    - All you have to do is focus on breathing. Easy peasy…in theory, anyway. You may find just focusing on breathing and sitting with your thoughts more challenging than you imagined. Sit in a quiet, calm spot and practice, practice, practice!

- **Practice deep breathing.**

    - Your breath will always guide you in emotionally charged situations. When you breathe, make sure that the exhalation is longer than the inhalation. It calms both the nervous system and the mind.

    - **Daniel Tiger**, a cartoon based on **Mr. Rogers'** iconic early childhood teachings, instructs viewers, "If you feel so mad that you want to roar, take a deep breath and count to four." While this message is intended for children, it's a much-needed reminder for adults too! Don't forget to breathe and take your time while doing it. You may just be surprised how shallow your natural breath can be when you're not aware of it. Channel lessons from early childhood friends to help regulate your emotions and remind you of universal truths.

- **Practice yoga**.

  - Yoga helps you practice being in the moment. And I'm not talking about fast, gym yoga with loud techno music. Find a slow, steady class where you can breathe into the stretches and focus on your mind and body sensations. Breathe deeply and master your thoughts. Yoga will make you more present so you release tension in your body, access higher levels of consciousness, and approach life more consciously (win, win, win). Or yin, yin, yin!

- **Spend time in nature**.

  - "Touch grass," as the kids say. Get out of your head and off your screen(s). Go outside.

  - Nature is the great healer. It helps reduce blood pressure, improves immune health, promotes better sleep, lowers stress hormone levels, and actually speeds up healing time (Hass, 2021). And it's lovely and free! So, hug a tree today. Say hello to a cardinal. Pet a dog. These are vibe-elevating activities!

Author **Eckhart Tolle** wrote in *A New Earth: Awakening to Your Life's Purpose*, "Whenever you interact with people, don't be there primarily as a function or a role, but as the field of conscious **Presence**. You can only lose something that you have, but you cannot lose something that you are."

As *Lesson 3—Improve your communication*—explores, active or empathic listening helps ground you in the present. It enables you to focus on the other person—*and really listen*—rather than zoning out and waiting for your turn to talk.

What else can you do to be present? When you feel triggered, stop, give yourself time to process, and engage your resources before you react.

- Check in with yourself
- Journal your thoughts
- Spend time in nature
- Call a neutral third party
- Talk to your therapist
- Read a book on communication or conflict
- Watch an educational video on conflict resolution

Be aware. Don't let unchecked emotions take over your life. Check in with yourself regularly and see the effect it will have on how you react to others around you. Know how to regulate your emotions to create the life you've always wanted for yourself.

The more grounded you are, the better your chances of reaching resolutions to the challenges in your life.

It starts with you.

Takeaways

In this chapter, we learned:

- People often choose **silence or violence** when they start to feel psychologically unsafe in a conversation, as we learn from *Crucial Conversations*.

- **"Silence"** is masking, avoiding, and withdrawing from conflict. **"Violence"** refers to controlling, labeling, and attacking when faced with conflict. Engaging in either of these styles will not resolve conflict in a healthy way.

- To get a handle on your emotions, journal your feelings, watch a video on conflict resolution or meditative exercises, step away, take a walk, practice yoga, or reach out to your therapist.

- Our basic functioning system is the **lizard brain**, which includes the brain stem, cerebellum, and basal ganglia. This older, less developed part of our brains takes over in emotional or stressful situations.

- Move out of the lizard brain and into the **prefrontal cortex** to engage your brain to make the best decisions by ensuring that your emotions don't overtake your thinking. If you've had trauma during your childhood, this will affect how your prefrontal cortex developed.

- Being **aware** of your journey and how it's impacted your brain development will help you overcome some of the habits you've created.

- The most **neutral** person in the room is the most powerful. Take time, breathe deeply, and get curious about a situation before letting your emotions take over. Stop your monkey mind from taking over.

- Calm your **monkey mind**—your noisy stream of consciousness—through yoga, education, deep breathing, journaling, therapy, and time in nature.

Self-Reflection Activity

Instructions: *Sit and reflect. Reflect on how you show up at work and beyond. Get comfortable and find uninterrupted time and a quiet space. Really give yourself space and time to reflect deeply.* Think about your conflict resolution style.

Q: How do I describe my conflict resolution style?

_____

_____

_____

_____

_____

_____

_____

_____

_____

_____

_____

_____

_____

_____

_____

_____

_____

_____

_____

_____

Q: In an emotional, stressful situation, is my tendency "silence" or "violence" from a conflict resolution standpoint?

_____
_____
_____
_____
_____
_____
_____
_____
_____
_____
_____
_____
_____
_____
_____
_____
_____
_____
_____
_____
_____
_____
_____
_____
_____
_____
_____

Q: Looking back at some conflicts objectively, what could I have done differently?

Next Steps

Extra Credit: Practice deep breathing the next time you feel angry in a conversation. Be mindful of how you engage and your emotional state before responding.

See how it impacts your next conflict.

Return to this exercise when a conflict is looming.

Search for meditative playlists on YouTube or Spotify.

Read on to discover the next lesson—**Manage your expectations.**

Lesson #5: Manage your expectations.

*"Tell your **CEO** your deepest, darkest secrets. It's okay. He's really embracing vulnerability this quarter, you guys. We're even reading—and quoting—a new book by the newest TED Talk darling. This is a **safe place** because **we're a family here**—the safest space ever. Until layoffs…**Or we decide you aren't a fit**…Or we stack rank you based on assumptions and biases (even though we totally have a training for that)...Or until you say something weird. But don't worry, silly! It wasn't what you shared at the offsite when we pressured you to be vulnerable. It was something…else. And we celebrate diversity! Unless you're from someplace weird that interferes with our interests. Then, we will gaslight and ignore you, and show you that you're not important to us while using your image on our diversity page because inclusion is sooooo important to us.*

*Love ya, TTYL! Signed, **Leading Leaders Who Lead**"*

Sound familiar?

Today's workplace is going through an **identity crisis**. It wants to be "hip" and "with it," as the kids say. It's trying to adapt and evolve to its employees' rapidly changing needs in a world that's evolving at warp speed. The workplace seems like it's trying to be everything to everyone. A place for all your hopes and dreams. An authentic, safe space! That's like a family! (*But, who said a family was safe?!*) Inclusive! Embraces diversity! (*Never mind the optics of our C-suite…there's diversity in our Diversity group!*).

Who needs a spiritual practice when we have capitalism to consume our minds and hearts as well?! And who needs *work-life balance* when you can have work-life *integration*? Don't separate your personal and professional lives! Just mush it all together in one big grab bag o' nonstop working/existing fun.

Leaders within the modern workplace have embraced teachings from thought leaders that promote **authenticity, vulnerability, and empathy**—outwardly, at least. While the workplace quickly adopted these leadership concepts, did this actually affect the environment? Has anything actually improved for employees? Or is the promise of these concepts just more *gaslighting* for employees? Have these concepts actually improved employees' well-being?

Here are some ways to **manage your expectations and protect your sanity** amid a sea of workplace doublespeak.

Boundaries Are Our Friends

Boundaries are limits we set through words and actions (Sanok, 2022). Healthy boundaries are always a good idea, no matter the setting. Think of the main character of the children's classic book *The Giving Tree* by Shel Silverstein.

In the tale, a loving tree **sacrifices every aspect of itself** for a boy-turned-man who takes and takes from the tree until it has nothing left to give him. While there are mixed feelings about the meaning behind this story, the moral is that while the tree is well-intentioned, it doesn't have healthy boundaries with the boy. Ultimately, the boy takes advantage of the tree's unconditional love and kindness.

This tale is referenced as a metaphor for everything from the environment to parenthood—although I would encourage any parents to avoid modeling themselves after a boundary-less stump! When it comes to the workplace, this kind of one-sided devotion and martyrdom is simply not necessary or healthy.

Don't be "The Giving Tree" at your work.

Do discover the boundaries that you want to uphold.

Focus on what you want and what you don't want.

Do create the circumstances you need to feel comfortable in the world.

Everybody Be Cool!

Employees are now advocating for their needs rather than accepting the status quo and holding on until retirement. According to the Bureau of Labor Statistics, the median for American workers staying at one job is **4.1 years** (Bureau of Labor, 2022).

When employees are not getting those needs met, they are moving on. You don't have to wait until you've given all your branches away.

Your Workplace *Isn't* a Family

You may have been told that your workplace is a family. But, here's some tough love…As much as the workplace aims to be transformational, it's *not your family*. *It's not your salvation.* The CEO is <u>not</u> your spiritual guru. No matter how much you love your job, organization, or teammates, **the workplace will not love you back**….unless you work in your family business.

The workplace is a place of employment where consent on either end can be revoked at ANY time. No matter what your company says. Comparing a company to a family is now being recognized as a red flag by prospective employees. (Bavin, 2023)

When many employees hear "We're a family," it doesn't evoke the same sentiment for each person. Many people are in therapy because of their actual families.

Why would I want to engage in more unhealthy dynamics where the boundaries are blurred because of love and obedience? I don't want a manager who is a wacky uncle; similarly, I don't want to repeat the familial archetypes such as the **hero, mascot, lost child/black sheep, or rescuer** (Pomerance, 2021).

Don't get lulled into the family dynamics. That concept makes people do things and act in ways they wouldn't if they had more firm boundaries: We are your employer; you are our employee; these are your colleagues. There's nothing wrong with that. Some of our colleagues can turn into lifelong friends. It all depends.

On the **Content People** podcast, author of *Disentangling from Emotionally Immature People,* **Dr. Lindsay C. Gibson** shares, "It's not hard to end up in work situations where you are doing a lot of the same things you're doing in your childhood…Certain family histories will make you more susceptible to being taken advantage of. Domineering or manipulative behavior may feel natural to you and it unconsciously feels like a dynamic you're destined to be a part of" (Farley, 2023).

You may find yourself trying to "prove" yourself to your manager/leader who replicates the Dad or Mom figure in your life. If you have unhealed family dynamics, this could be very dangerous emotionally! It can cause you to become enmeshed and entangled with your workplace in ways that don't serve your professional journey or mental health.

Robert Jackson says, "There's a good chance you're more likely to act like a martyr for your work-family, which can have serious implications for your real family. Instead, workplaces should just focus on getting cool shit done, being real, and making sure people are being rewarded appropriately."

Humans Are Emotional

Humans are gonna human. It's not just **Whitney Houston** who gets so emotional *(baby)*, as the old song goes, but also people in the workplace. Many aspects of the workplace are emotional. No matter where you land, (unless you work for robots), you will have to deal with humans—*sorry*! And humans are messy. They judge and hold grudges. They can be cranky and arbitrary. They play favorites (Perry, 2023).

Humans say they are working on their biases while actively engaging in their favorite ones. They can bring their unhealed trauma and dump it all over whoever is closest to them.

Many **Black and Brown employees** know this all too well. They're told to bring their authentic selves to work, but in a way that is acceptable to their employer, which varies from organization to organization.

Disclaimer: Human beings can also be very lovely as well.

Don't be shocked when human emotions catch up with you in the workplace! Even when people say they are evolved, self-aware, advocates for diversity, and everything they think they *should* say, this is not always the case. Everything is subjective. That includes empathy.

Empathy Is Subjective

Your **empathy** and *my* empathy may be completely different.

Empathetic concepts have saturated LinkedIn, business books, and articles in recent years. It's gotten to the point where those words have lost all meaning. The folks that get it, get it. And the ones that don't...well...if the workplace has to teach you about empathy, it might be hard to learn as a fully formed adult (*looking at you, Erika Jane from The Real Housewives of Beverly Hills*) (O'Brien, 2023).

According to *Harvard Business Review,* when leaders do things like responding to failure with *artificial compassion* and inauthentically ask for *feedback* without acting on it, that's **fake psychological safety** (Carucci, 2023).

Empathetic people empathized with others before it was cool. They understood and related to other people's emotions before ROI or leadership skills were associated with it.

Many empathetic people had to learn to calcify their hearts to protect themselves from people who see **kindness as a weakness** (no matter how many articles claim otherwise).

As someone who takes words literally, I will admit that I tend to naively believe people's words and take them literally in my career. So, I was shocked when the words and the actions did not align. I remember reading and re-reading a playbook from a company when things started getting weird. "Wait a minute, our core value says we value honesty, but this person is demonstrating the opposite of that value and getting rewarded for it!" I was trying to make sense of the documented guidelines versus what was happening in real life. It wasn't adding up. It confused and frustrated me and many others. I've since realized that *everyone's lived experience is different, so they perceive their actions differently*. Chances are, someone's definition of a value or attribute may not line up with yours. I had to learn that the answers weren't as simple as flipping to page 47 of the guidebook.

Oftentimes, there's a **disconnect between what's said and what's done**. If you've been in the workplace, I'm sure you've noticed the difference. "Do as I say, not as I do." Many employees are told that their input is welcome at their workplace but don't have an outlet to share it. Or when they do and it's not the "right" input or there's backlash. They're labeled "disrupters," "problematic," or worse "unhappy." Nowadays, emotionally unsafe people in the workplace can weaponize empathy to manipulate and gaslight you. Everything you say and do can and will be used against you. It's possible that an unwell person manipulates it for their own gain.

As we learned in *Lesson 3—Improve your communication* and *Lesson 4—Understand your conflict style*, understanding best practices in communication and conflict resolution can help you mitigate the messiness of human interaction.

Advocate for Yourself

"Speak up, girl!"

This is the passionate advice the late, great CEO and founder of a company I worked for—gave me. He sat across from me in a cubicle in the company's headquarters for many years in the 2010s. To me, he was like a combination of Chuck Norris, The Most Interesting Man in the World, a no-nonsense construction dude, and a hippie. A business hippie, actually.

As the leader of a flat organization, he wanted to show his employees that he didn't need a fancy office; he wanted to sit amongst his people in the open office environment. *(Although if I were him, you better believe I'd have the nice office with the door SHUT, but props to him for wanting to be amongst his people.)* I was lucky to absorb some of his empathetic yet straightforward leadership in action.

One day, we were having a random conversation. After I casually mentioned how I wanted a sit-stand desk for a long time, he told me "Speak up, girl!"

If I wanted something, why not ask? That encouragement stayed with me over the years. *Why had I silenced myself and not asked for what I wanted?* It was a simple enough ask. The truth is I didn't want to rock the boat or draw attention to myself as high maintenance.

No one wants to be like Milton from the classic workplace film 1999's *Office Space*: meek, forgettable, and muttering about his stolen stapler…until the end of the movie of course (spoiler alert), which is not exactly an ethical resolution to Milton's conflict (Judge, 1999).

Vulnerability Is Not for Everyone

Your workplace and leadership are not immune to trends. While the tide has shifted to buzzwords like **empathy and vulnerability**, some employees resent being forced to open up and even cry in front of each other.

Are you already pretty open, or are you more selective in what you share and with whom you share it? This is a spectrum and it varies from organization to organization. Do you save your deeper emotional engagement for friends and family and find it exhausting to perform strong emotions on cue in the workplace?

Unfortunately, vulnerability is not for everyone. Don't get confused by the *Harvard Business Review* articles and the like that shout at you about vulnerability. The C-suite can be vulnerable and you can probably be vulnerable with people you can trust (maybe), but *not everyone*. It can backfire when "non-leaders" open up. That vulnerability can and will be used against you. It can be used to question your competence, wellness, or work ethic.

Host of the podcast *Content People* and CEO of Medbury, a social media agency, **Meredith Farley** offers the following alternative: "Instead of vulnerability, we should be able to expect **judicious transparency**. Instead of empathy, we should be able to expect **thoughtful consideration**. Very few people have the right pitch of their tuning fork for empathy."

Not everyone wants to share their trauma with their teammates just because the latest facilitator wants to force group bonding on you. You may be labeled a certain way that comes back on your *performance review* because of something you shared. If you share something personal with your manager, know that it may be weaponized against you when they share it with *their* manager. Sometimes, less is more.

Therapist and trainer **Tiffany Totah** says, "Vulnerability in the workplace has gone too far, creating emotional unsafety for people. You have these offsites or summits where an organization wants you to be vulnerable and emotional, which can be uncomfortable. Then they learn too much, making people want to care for others emotionally. I'm not an advocate for vulnerability in the workplace, but I'm an advocate for supporting each person's journey."

When people are pressured to be **vulnerable**, especially in toxic cultures of dynamics, this creates a lot of emotional and psychological distress for employees.

*Nancy—a mid-career marketing specialist[1]—shared the following experience: "I was at a meeting at my toxic job. They pressured us to share personal struggles in our lives. Someone on my team led the exercise. And I didn't trust her to begin with! I was so uncomfortable. I'd always taught myself to protect my sensitivity. I'm an open book outside of work, but this was work! And dynamics were incredibly odd and draining on this team. There were constant power struggles. I was working with people that were out for themselves. While they felt safe to open up because they felt protected by their mentors or sponsors in leadership, I felt pressured and without any protection from a mentor or sponsor. It felt emotionally manipulative and I left the company shortly afterward."

Look to *Lesson 6—Be your own workplace BFF* for more on how to advocate for yourself.

---

[1] Name has been changed to protect identity

Safety Is a Spectrum

Psychological safety is "the ability to feel safe acknowledging failure, offering tough feedback, sharing unorthodox ideas, and telling the truth about difficult situations without fear of retaliation" (Markish, 2023).`

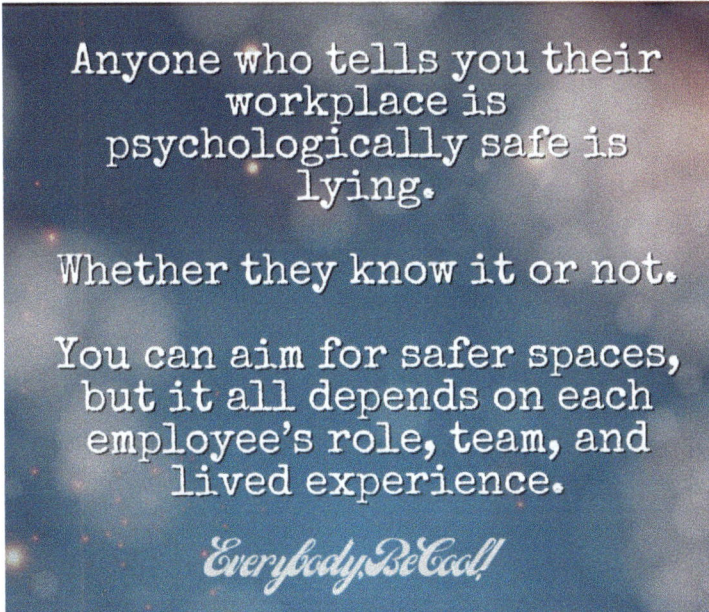

> Anyone who tells you their workplace is psychologically safe is lying.
>
> Whether they know it or not.
>
> You can aim for safer spaces, but it all depends on each employee's role, team, and lived experience.
>
> *Everybody Be Cool!*

According to *Harvard Business Review,* there can be dire consequences for a lack of psychological safety in the workplace as demonstrated in 1986's Challenger and 2003's Columbia Space Shuttle disasters. These crashes led to fatalities of the crews onboard. While employees did raise concerns before the crashes, NASA did not heed their warnings, which would have avoided the disasters (Carucci, 2023). These examples serve as sobering reminders of the importance of the **employee voice** in the workplace.

Psychological safety has to be authentic for it to work—not just lip service! When leaders respond to failure with *artificial compassion* and inauthentically ask for *feedback without* acting on it, that is regarded as **fake psychological safety.**

Remember that consent can be taken away on either end at any time and that your working relationship can end. Leadership's version of **safety** may not align with yours. In the workplace, everything you do or say will be held against you, no matter the latest trends or the written policies.

It depends on who you are and what is happening in the universe. Just because someone utters the words, *"This is a safe space,"* does not magically make it safe. What's been done to make said space "safe?"

We can't know what's in someone's mind or heart. Anyone with social anxiety will tell you that a place with more than one human being is no longer safe. Group dynamics are not safe. Heck, group *chats* are not safe. Anyone can erupt at any moment. Anything can be misconstrued. How someone's behavior is tolerated depends on their status in the group and the culture surrounding it. Group therapy is one thing, work is another.

You can aim for a *safer* space, but a <u>safe</u> space? It's not a realistic expectation unless the world goes through a massive spiritual shift, which we still await.

But remember, the shift can start within <u>you</u>! While you don't have to be obligated to share things you're uncomfortable sharing, your confidence and boundary-setting can cause a shift to create a safer, truly authentic workplace culture.

Takeaways

In this chapter, we learned:

- **Boundaries are your friends.**
  - Don't be a professional version of *The Giving Tree* and give away all your branches until you're just a stump (mentally and emotionally). Protecting yourself and looking out for your spiritual and emotional development is okay at work—even ideal!

- **Your workplace *isn't* a family.**
  - Using familial terms is unhealthy in the workplace. It sets up unrealistic expectations and can bring up triggering dynamics. Avoid getting emotionally entangled or confused if your workplace uses these terms.

- **Humans are emotional.**
  - While people can think of themselves as emotionally intelligent or empathetic, their actions don't always line up. Remember that emotions and human frailty will often cloud interactions in the workplace.

- **Empathy is subjective.**
  - Since everyone's lived experience is different, everyone's definition of empathy is different. Some people are naturally empathetic. Some talk the talk but don't embody it. Some must learn how to become empathetic. It will look and feel different depending on the person.

- **Advocate for yourself.**
  - ○ Speak up. Don't expect others to read your mind and magically give you what you want. Ask for it. The worst that can happen is that someone says no. Asking for what you want shows that you aren't afraid to try.

- **Vulnerability is not for everyone.**
  - ○ If you don't feel comfortable sharing something personal during a company function, don't feel pressured to share it. Share what you are comfortable sharing and say what feels safe. Vulnerability is a privilege, and it's not always safe to be vulnerable at work, depending on your role and organization.

- **Safety is a spectrum.**
  - ○ Just because someone says a space is safe doesn't make it so. Organizations can aim for a *safer space* by implementing measures to achieve it. Have realistic expectations about what's possible at work.

Self-Reflection Activity

Instructions: *Sit and reflect. Reflect on how you show up at work and beyond. Get comfortable and find uninterrupted time and a quiet space. Really give yourself space and time to reflect deeply. Think about your expectations in your career.*

Q: *How have emotions shown up in my career?* This could be from managers or colleagues you've worked with or your own. What emotions were rewarded and what were penalized?

_____

_____

_____

_____

_____

_____

_____

_____

_____

_____

_____

_____

_____

_____

_____

_____

_____

_____

_____

_____

Q: *How has vulnerability shown up in my career?* Did I ever share and regret opening up? What did I learn from that?

_____
_____
_____
_____
_____
_____
_____
_____
_____
_____
_____
_____
_____
_____
_____
_____
_____
_____
_____
_____
_____
_____
_____
_____
_____
_____
_____
_____

Q: *What's one expectation I had in my career that did not come true?* What did I learn from that?

_____
_____
_____
_____
_____
_____
_____
_____
_____
_____
_____
_____
_____
_____
_____
_____
_____
_____
_____
_____
_____

Next Steps

Read on to the next and final lesson—**Be your own workplace BFF**.

Lesson #6: Be your own workplace BFF.

Does your role fit your spirit? Are you a pacifist working for a weapons manufacturer? PETA enthusiast working for Cruella de Vil?

Don't work in a role or for an organization that's against your values. It's not worth it. If your personal and company values are at odds with each other, that's a big **red flag**. And that's going to majorly impact your well-being. Move away from something that does not sit right within your spirit and find opportunities that align.

While it's important to be open to evolution, your foundational beliefs and values should be your core. If your actions align with your values and beliefs but you are still unsatisfied, consider how you can create a win-win for yourself and your workplace.

How can you do that?

Be your own workplace **best friend forever (BFF)**! A workplace BFF **advocates** for you, **advises** you, **cheers** you on, and **looks out** for you. They genuinely want the best for you. Your bestie is not looking to compete with you. They check in with you and send you funny GIFs to cheer you up when you're having a tough day. They make you look forward to coming to work (even if it's remote). Their support texts and calls are everything.

I've luckily had several workplace BFFs in my life. These empathetic, brilliant, and amazing souls (shoutout to them) have helped me through many challenging and uncool times. Some can even become lifelong friends long after we leave the organizations we trauma-bonded over.

Reflect on <u>your</u> workplace BFF (past or present) if you've been lucky enough to find one. *How did that person talk to you? Did they help you see a situation in a different way? Did they find opportunities for you that you weren't aware of? Did they remind you of your strengths?*

Be that for <u>yourself</u>. If you've never had one at work, think of your BFF in life and pretend you are them. As *your own BFF*, give yourself the encouragement you'd give to your friend. Replace telling your BFF "you can do it" with telling *yourself* "I can do it."

How you **speak to yourself** determines many outcomes in your life. It will make all the difference in your beliefs about what you can do and how you should be treated. When you become your own best friend, you can **navigate culture, direct your career,** and **manage your personal brand** while serving yourself and your workplace—present and future. Make it clear who you are and your worth so you won't be overlooked and undervalued.

Navigating Culture

Is culture another way to describe "the vibes?"

Like a living, breathing organism, culture is the sum <u>total of its parts</u>. Each individual in a workplace adds (or detracts) from that culture. And **you** are a vital part of any group you belong to (place of worship, family, friends, local community, workplace, etc.). Like life, the workplace brings together all types of people. You likely relate to some of your coworkers better than others.

According to *Gallup:* "Few things are as important -- and sometimes as difficult to grasp -- as an organization's culture." A lot of organizational culture is about how people get things done.

There are *three parts of culture*:

1. **The organization**
2. **Leadership**
3. **The individual**

#1—The Organization

Culture is *more* than the stated *core values* on a website or a few paragraphs of boilerplate text on a company's intranet. It's easy to say "We believe in bunnies and unicorns and Care Bears," but reality is another thing. It's about which behaviors organizations tolerate and who they promote, how people communicate, and how different treatment is permitted based on status and power.

> **"ORGANIZATIONS CAN BE TOXIC.**
>
> WHAT'S DIFFICULT IS WHEN IT'S SEEMINGLY GREAT FROM THE OUTSIDE, BUT ON THE INSIDE, IT'S NOT.
>
> EVERYONE SEEMS HAPPY BUT IN REALITY, NO ONE WANTS TO ROCK THE BOAT."
>
> Christina Dyer

And it varies by each individual and their unique lived experience. It's what's unspoken. It's how meetings are run.

It's how decisions are made. And it might not always be what it seems. The longer you're at an organization, your view of the culture may change. It may not be obvious. It could seem like a harmonious, productive culture but little by little, you may start to see puzzling or toxic aspects of the culture.

Or the culture itself may change as circumstances change. It may not scale as the company grows.

#2—Leadership

A company's chosen leadership team (also known as *Leading Leaders Who Lead*) plays a significant role in creating, modeling, and accepting tolerated or unacceptable behaviors. Does leadership follow a "Do as I say not as I do" policy? *How do they handle reports of workplace bullying?* You may find that the "rules" are ever-changing, depending on who is involved and intangible factors like *favoritism, status*, and *power*.

While a harmonious workplace utopia may certainly be the intention in corporate culture, that's not usually the case in reality.

What do you do in an organization where people say one thing but do another? *Is it okay for Jimmy to power-play Suzie?* Does that make him a "straight shooter with upper management written all over him?" Culture is, after all, subjective. But when the words and daily reality differ, it can feel like **gaslighting**.

No matter the culture, it's important not to get lost in your organization's shuffle.

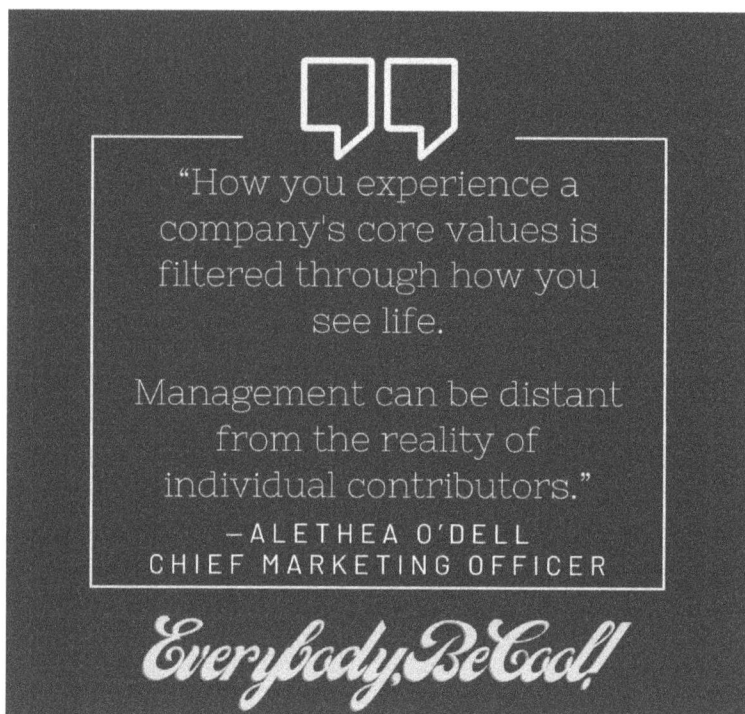

> "How you experience a company's core values is filtered through how you see life.
>
> Management can be distant from the reality of individual contributors."
>
> —ALETHEA O'DELL
> CHIEF MARKETING OFFICER
>
> *Everybody, Be Cool!*

#3—The Individual

It's not just leadership or the organization alone that impacts culture. The third part of culture is the individual. Aside from an organization's purpose, each individual has a *purpose* that informs how they see their role, work, and, ultimately, life! You are the only one who can decide how you will "show up" at work (and in life). And workplace culture is a collection of **individuals coming together and agreeing on ways of being together.**

That's pretty deep!

That perspective gives each employee more power than they may think they have. You don't have to view yourself as a cog in the wheel of "the machine" that you rage against.

How **you** decide to show up in the workplace directly impacts your coworkers, their families, and their communities in a ripple effect. What we choose to speak about and focus on, how we resolve conflict, how we talk to ourselves—all of these factors impact the whole.

Messy work situations can feel so overwhelming that the stress seeps into your personal life. It's hard to compartmentalize and suddenly become a happy, patient, energized person ready to engage with kids, spouses, friends, or even yourself once the clock strikes 5 pm (or 6 pm or midnight). You may find that your work stress causes you to feel depleted, on edge, and angry at home. And that serves no one.

Do you want to have the same problems manifesting repeatedly, *no matter your workplace*? No, you don't.

Here's what you can do to make the most of your blood, sweat, and tears in the workplace and the culture of your organization:

- Don't get lost in the shuffle
- Direct your career
- Develop your personal brand
- Get a mentor, sponsor, or both
- Write your book

Don't Get Lost in the Shuffle

Everyone in the workplace knows how they are showing up...*Nope!*

Not even close. You may deal more with people's unhealed issues in the workplace than *actual work*. Once you understand this, it will make things clearer in your career, especially for conflict-avoidant folks.

Rivalries are concocted. People play mind games. They make power plays. Unwell people find themselves in positions of authority and wreak havoc.

The workplace can mirror *Game of Thrones* but with more zip-up vests. *Have you ever experienced a "red wedding"-level power struggle at work?* They're not pretty. That cut-throat corporate behavior is what many people saw modeled, as we learned in Lesson 1—*Be aware of your surroundings*. Many people are operating on myths and beliefs that are vastly different from the standard business models and trends we see today.

And more often than not, the people in your organization are too busy **Games-of-Thronesing** each other to be focused on you—even the leaders. Especially the leaders. They focus on *their* careers, power plays, and disputes. You, unfortunately, may not be on their radar. Or they may not see you how you want them to, no matter how hard you work to prove yourself.

Leadership & Advancement Dynamics

Many **high-performing individual contributors** may shy away from advancing their careers or pursuing leadership opportunities for many reasons, which could include:

- "Icky" corporate politics
- Juggling other priorities, such as caretaking or commitments outside of work
- Lack of encouragement for introverts or neurodiverse employees
- Advancement doesn't seem appealing or worth the effort
- They want to focus on their specialty rather than manage others
- There's no clear path to leadership for them

Just because you're not in an official leadership position at work doesn't mean you're *not* a leader. You can be a role model for your colleagues. You can be a leader outside of work in your community, amongst your friends, or within your family.

In this new era's emphasis on consciousness, being **unconscious** (or unaware, as we learned in Lesson 2—*Journey into your awareness*) in the workplace can be even more of a hindrance than in past decades. As more people in the workplace name these toxic traits, it becomes less acceptable. But still, some of the most unconscious people can use (and weaponize) words like **empathy** and **consciousness**. They can even **teach communication training.** And they can feel invincible because they are a leader (you know, the all-important "Leading Leader Who Leads") or "favorite" of someone powerful in the organization.

No one can FORCE someone to look within their hearts and make a change. That has to come from the individual. An unaware person will remain unaware if their behavior works for them or if the story they tell themselves paints them as the hero.

Not every leader will be like *Succession*'s fictional cranky billionaire Logan Roy, making their inner circle play a humiliating game called "Boar on the Floor" to find the traitor amongst the group. It is usually more subtle—and more confusing (Kornhaber & Beck, 2019).

Before investing too much of your heart and soul in one organization, make sure you have a realistic view of the actual circumstances and not the *idealized view* that the organization wants you to believe in. Life is short.

> **"IF YOU FEEL ENERGETICALLY OUT OF ALIGNMENT, TRUST YOUR INSTINCTS...**
>
> **IF THE VIBES ARE OFF, I'M OUT."**
>
> — MEREDITH FARLEY, CEO & PODCAST HOST

EverybodyBeCool

This helps temper any unrealistic ideals you may have about your organization. It's too much pressure. You never know what kind of organization you end up in. It can start as one thing and then change. This is **your life** we're talking about. And you only get one of those bad boys (as far as we know). That's why it's essential to direct YOUR career yourself rather than getting caught up in the whims of your organization. Always **keep your goals in mind**.

I'll admit I've gotten caught up at organizations where I've left it up to them to decide where they want to put me. *"You tell me where I should go, guys!"* This is a passive and chaotic approach. And it wastes time and undermines your power. Trust yourself. Get clear on what you want and direct your career where you want it to go, rather than hoping someone sees what you are meant to do.

Direct Your Career

Host of the podcast *Content People* and CEO of Medbury, **Meredith Farley** says, "I used to think, 'If you just work and work and are an extra hard team player, one day leadership will notice and give you a special award!' That's not always true for everyone. Some people are in the wrong roles, at the wrong organization, and have no path for advancement or no clear path to success in their role! They mistakenly think if they work harder, go above and beyond, and keep putting in 120% year after year, they'll miraculously get noticed. That's not usually the case."

It's also important to know when your organization and you are out of sync to the point of no return. As Kenny Rogers famously said in the '80s classic song *The Gambler*, "You gotta know when to hold 'em, know when to fold 'em." It's helpful to know what you *don't want* as much as knowing what you do want. This helps you focus.

People are going to **see you from their lived perspective**. In the workplace, you will be leveraged for your skills. That's part of the process. It's transactional by design. And to advance in your career, someone (often the one leveraging your skills) has to advocate for you. They might not see you in the way you want to be seen.

Don't wait for your leadership or organization to ordain you "Special-est of the Specials.**" Ordain yourself in your mindset and mentality. Your mentality follows you no matter the organization.**

Life's too short to let yourself get blown along the corporate winds like the "most beautiful" plastic bag from the 1999 film *American Beauty.* Direct your future instead of hoping someone will just "get" you or automatically understand how you can contribute to their bottom line. Remember that since it is transactional from the organization's perspective, it can be transactional from your perspective if you are not getting what you want from the experience.

Not all of us are "gettable" without spelling it out for people. Marketing is all about repetition and for people to understand your strengths, you must keep repeating it in different ways—in person and online.

That's where personal branding comes in. That's where you can really be your own BFF and hype yourself by making it explicitly clear what your strengths are and how you want to be seen.

Develop Your Personal Brand

How do you build your personal brand?

Tell your story. No one can tell your story like you. Your story is your personal brand. Some of you may cringe at the phrase "personal brand." I get it. We are human beings. Do we have to be brands now, too?

Think of your personal brand as your **reputation**. You have one whether you like it or not. *How do you want people to think of you?* Yes, you are being perceived, as uncomfortable as that may be. It's just a matter of nudging your perception in the direction you want. Don't let people concoct it for you. They may not understand the intricacies of your role or your skillset. Others may have developed an assumption about you based on *their lived experience or biases.*

Maybe you trigger them or remind them of someone. They will tell your narrative how *they* see it. **The stronger the narrative you create about your personal brand (reputation), the more that can speak for itself rather than others' interpretations.**

Become a LinkedIn Power User

You must sing your praises in your career. There's no getting around that. One major way to brand yourself is through **LinkedIn**—the number-one professional social networking platform with over one billion users. You've probably used LinkedIn at a bare minimum to add to your professional experience or apply for jobs. But if you're not keeping up, **LinkedIn is more than just a digital resume**. It's evolved into a social media ecosystem that forges friendships, teaches new skills, and empowers people from all walks of life. And it connects people.

Even my nephew who is still in high school is on LinkedIn; he's way ahead of the game. It's never too late. Don't let a teenager beat you to it! If he can do it, so can you.

If you're unsure how to interact on LinkedIn, get comfortable with regularly logging in to the platform and observing the type of content and creators you're interested in. You can watch tutorials on best practices on LinkedIn Learning or YouTube. It's like a muscle. The more you use it, the stronger it gets.

How can you get started?

Connect, comment, react! Post about what you know and what you've done. Post regularly. Interact with others in your network and beyond.

Consider sharing a lesson you learned in your career, an insight, or something you'd share with someone at a networking event. Here's where you can be a corporate Flavor Flav that shouts your name and ability. No one will be more excited about you than you.

Find **like-minded people** and/or people you can learn from or grow with. Support each other. Share that enthusiasm with your LinkedIn buddies by engaging with their content and encouraging them on their journeys. Pay it forward.

I'm grateful that after getting laid off, I found a supportive community of content creators who encouraged me and cheered me on. They'd comment and react to my posts and I'd do the same for them. And some even became my friends IRL (in real life). It's a nice reminder that there are people out there who we can connect to on different topics and interests.

Cher Jones, a personal branding trainer, strategist, content creator, speaker, and LinkedIn Learning instructor, says, "Posting on LinkedIn gives us a unique opportunity to **reframe and refocus how people see us**. Your content proves what you know, have done, and can do. It allows us to control the narrative. Your brand can do that for you if you put it to work. You can influence how people look and see and remember you."

Cher leverages many features of LinkedIn such as LinkedIn Live and Audio Events to speak to her 30,000 followers. She encourages her listeners to use their **content** to create the conversation they want and show proof of what they've done.

> "The branded wheel gets the grease. It's a hard to ignore awesome.
>
> Leverage the success tool that is your brand.
>
> Let people know what you do, how you can help, and how they can trust you."
>
> **—Cher Jones**
> *Personal Branding Trainer*

Everybody, Be Cool!

Be your own hype person. This is where you can **"manifest"** what you want. *If you're not excited about you, who else will be?* And why <u>not</u> be excited about yourself? It's easy to be critical of yourself rather than give yourself credit. Look past the cringe and start flexing that muscle. It's just the way to do business these days. If you don't do this, others and their interpretation of you will do it for you, and it will probably be wrong.

You shouldn't have to fear being laid off if you are cultivating your personal brand and narrative. Expect that it may happen. You should be able to leverage your brand rather than reacting to bad news and then rushing to polish up your resume/professional presence online. Empower yourself by staying ready.

We breathe life into the things we say. Choose your words and your energy wisely. When we underplay our skills or ability, that may backfire, and colleagues may think we are less confident and therefore, less capable. And when many of your colleagues promote their personal brands, if you don't, then doing *nothing* is just as much of a statement as doing *something*. So, you might as well do something, right? Speak it into existence!

LinkedIn is not *just* for looking for a job. It places power in the hands of each employee. It lets YOU control your narrative. Not your manager or your organization's whims. Those can change on a dime. You are stuck with you for your entire career. Don't think of posting on LinkedIn as being a desperate weirdo looking for another job, think of it as building content to display your knowledge.

Known as "The Creator's Creator" on LinkedIn, **Isabel Sterne** is a hilarious writer, marketer, and brand strategist who uses humor, vulnerability, and relatability to encourage other creators to share their thought leadership online. She shares her reasoning for advocating for personal branding through platforms such as LinkedIn and Substack—an online publishing platform for newsletters.

> "**Everyone** should have a voice in the workplace!
>
> And it's not like that.
>
> It's extremely *hierarchical*.
>
> That drew me to **personal branding** because you have a **voice and a platform**. Companies can't mess with you when you have that."
>
> —Isabel Sterne
> Writer, Marketer, Branding Strategist
>
> *Everybody, Be Cool!*

Her humor and honesty resonate with her audience—fellow content creators trying and adjusting their strategy and being themselves while creating the career they want.

The hardest part is getting started. Get over the fear of judgment or failure. I've posted about movies, writing, mugs, coffee, dogs, Muppets, and everything else. People want a glimpse of you as a professional and as a person. This is your way to show them. Just start! If you reconsider, the edit function is there for a reason. Dip a toe in, embrace the awkwardness, and go for it.

Find Your Voice

What's your voice? Is it playful? Succinct? Descriptive? Relaxed?

According to Linkedin, your **personal brand is your value proposition**. Find out who you are professionally. Discover the attributes of your voice. And start sharing! You can always edit your posts. Get used to creating and maintaining your professional and personal brand with content on LinkedIn. Don't overthink it.

Think of **posting as an opportunity to share anecdotes or stories** as if you're networking with someone and having a great, interesting conversation. It just happens to be broadcasting to more than one person. Think of digital networking as **a win for introverts**. We introverts can show off our professional expertise and lovely personalities in a way that's *comfortable*—well, as much as it can be. Embrace the unknown and experiment.

I was never a fan of formalized in-person networking. I often hid in the bathroom until I found an extrovert to glom onto. While I love talking to people, the forced setting with a rotating rhythm stresses me out. I never know if I stay too long or short in a conversation. I also have sweaty hands, especially when I'm nervous or have to interact with humans, so it's very uncool for all involved.

Just Do It

Your LinkedIn **content doesn't have to be perfect**. It's *just* another social media outlet. But a little more proper because your company is linked (*get it?*) to your name. So, if you say something weird, it could affect your employment. But NO PRESSURE!

If you don't know where to start, share an **article** or **picture of your day at your job** or **interesting facts** about your field or profession. Or share that you are new to LinkedIn and open to suggestions for how to get started.

Think about your strengths, passions, and skills. Also consider your target audience—their needs, challenges, and desires. *In other words, what's your audience's deal?* Create a poll and ask your network a question.

I won't lie to you and tell you to be *exactly yourself* like many other articles, books, webinars, and speakers tell you. Some of us know too well that **we can't be our exact selves**, which is what it is. **Find as much of yourself as you're comfortable sharing and *lean into it.***

As you learned in Lesson 5—*Manage your expectations*, even when people constantly implore you to "be authentic," that's subjective. In the real world, being fully yourself and saying EXACTLY what you want to say may not always be a realistic option. For many reasons.

Vulnerability and authenticity depend on the context, power dynamics, and people involved. Social media connects our "work" and "personal" personas, whereas generations prior could separate the two more. Nowadays, everything is jumbled together. Your aunt, your manager, and your high school friends are all tied together through LinkedIn.

You don't have to share your diary with the world. Find a topic that interests you. Discover the level of openness you're comfortable with.

It may feel repetitive, but remember, people are consumed with their lives and not paying as much attention to you as you think. It takes time and different ways of saying the same thing before it clicks. *Ah yes, there's Layla! She's an HR specialist who leverages data and empathetic insights to achieve goals.* You go, Layla.

You may feel nervous to post because it might seem like you're looking for a new job and you don't want to alarm your colleagues that you're on the hunt. That's an outdated fear. It should be assumed that everyone is always looking (or open), even if casually so.

After all, if you got a better offer, why not consider it? Building your brand is not about searching for another job although sometimes that happens due to the work.

Being active on LinkedIn is also **good for your organization and your personal brand**, whether your organization realizes it or not. People with a strong presence on LinkedIn are a testament to their organization.

When employees have a strong LinkedIn presence, it shows that a company hires the best and brightest and empowers them to share their experiences, observations, perspectives, and personalities.

All those strong personal brands create an even stronger workplace culture because *their **voices unite and amplify each other***.

Be brave! Try something new. Have fun with it. You can always edit or delete.

Start building your content and your personal brand.

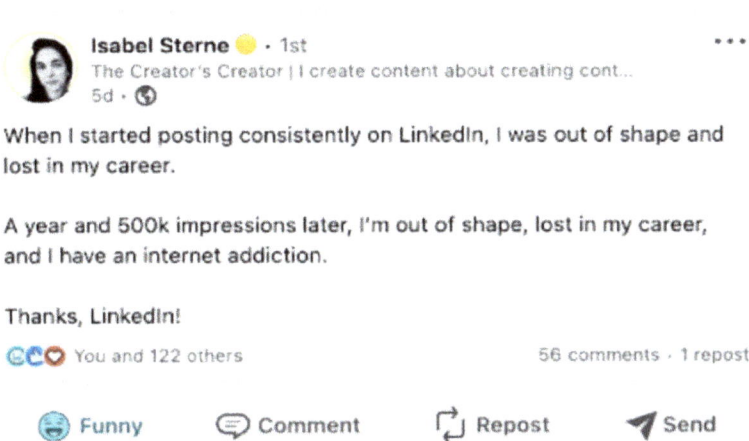

Isabel Sterne 🟡 · 1st
The Creator's Creator | I create content about creating cont...
5d · 🌐

When I started posting consistently on LinkedIn, I was out of shape and lost in my career.

A year and 500k impressions later, I'm out of shape, lost in my career, and I have an internet addiction.

Thanks, LinkedIn!

👍😊❤️ You and 122 others   56 comments · 1 repost

😄 Funny   💬 Comment   🔁 Repost   ➤ Send

Make the voice your own, as shown in this LinkedIn post. Humor is part of Isabel's voice, but find a tone that is authentic for <u>you</u>.

Find out what makes your voice and embrace it. Personal branding experts encourage posting on LinkedIn often and regularly.

As Cher Jones shares, "If you haven't done the work to brand yourself, you get what you get and you don't get upset."

Make friends! Worst/best case scenario, you make new friends through LinkedIn. Some of the coolest people I've met lately have been through LinkedIn. And it started with supporting each other's content. You'll find like-minded people the more you share and interact with others' posts!

Elevator Pitch

In addition to your LinkedIn posts, perfect your **30-second elevator pitch**. This is how you would describe your career and expertise if you were riding on an elevator with someone and had to sum it up in half a minute.

An elevator pitch makes it easy for people to understand you and your skills at a high-level.

Are you an excellent designer? Tech whiz? Great with data? Strategic problem solver? Fantastic flutist?

Figure out your story.

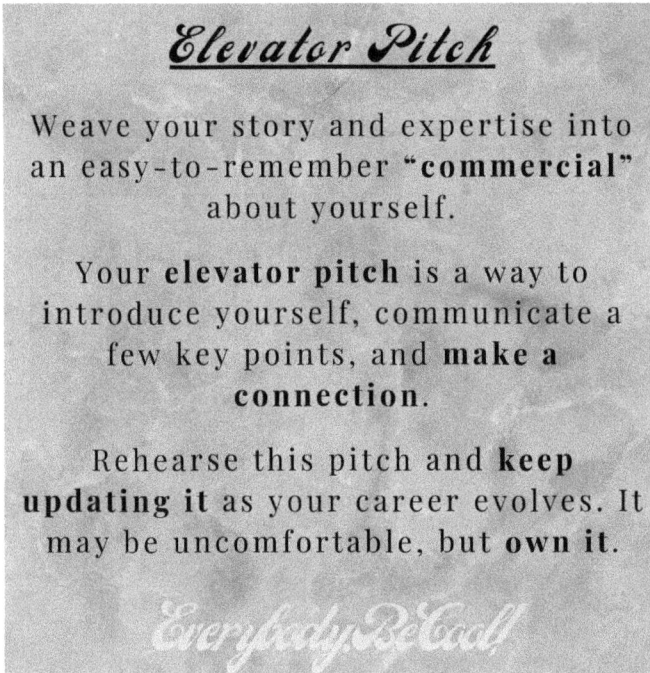

Elevator Pitch

Weave your story and expertise into an easy-to-remember **"commercial"** about yourself.

Your **elevator pitch** is a way to introduce yourself, communicate a few key points, and **make a connection.**

Rehearse this pitch and **keep updating it** as your career evolves. It may be uncomfortable, but **own it**.

Everybody Be Cool

The more comfortable you are with your elevator pitch, the better you can articulate what you offer. Your content exists online and in how you conduct yourself in person and online.

Are you showing up confidently and proudly? Or apologetic and unsure?

Make sure that you are seen how you want to be seen. And if you are not feeling sure of yourself, tap into your inner workplace BFF and keep hyping yourself up. **Ask your actual bestie.** Find skills you have that you may take for granted or underplay. If you are new to the workplace, focus on skills you can develop to take your career to the next level. Figure out who you are and shout it from the rooftops. *That's your BFF!*

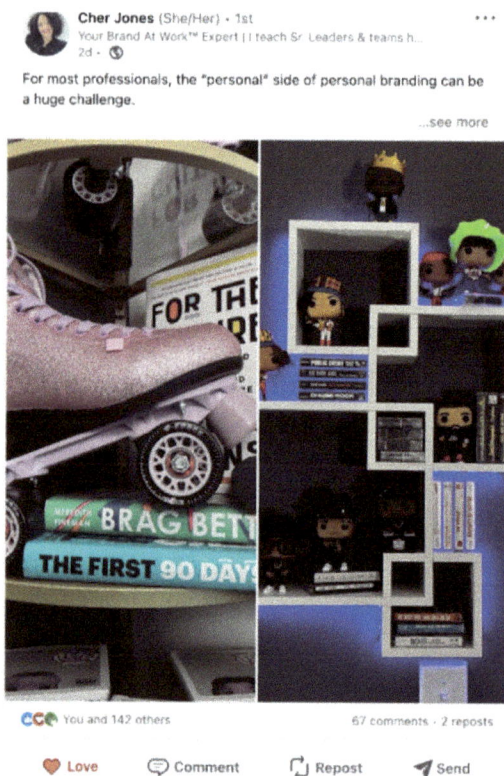

Cher Jones (She/Her) · 1st
Your Brand At Work™ Expert | I teach Sr. Leaders & teams h...
2d · 🌐

For most professionals, the "personal" side of personal branding can be a huge challenge.

...see more

😊😊😊 You and 142 others   67 comments · 2 reposts

💛 Love   💬 Comment   🔁 Repost   ➤ Send

In the LinkedIn post's shown on the previous page, Cher Jones shares how the visible items in your background on virtual calls can tell people more about you. She calls these visual cues the "Easter eggs" of your brand or "curated authenticity."
These items drop subtle hints about your interests and hobbies without oversharing. Cher's post shows her background, which consists of books, cassette tapes, a pink glittery roller skate, and Run DMC Funko POP! figures. Now that's a fun background! And it lets people know more about Cher when they are on a call with her. It's like her logo came to life—but more personal.

Network the New Way

Nowadays, **most networking occurs remotely**—a significant win for sweaty-handed people who dread the hand-shaking of networking events! I've made many friends and found jobs and opportunities through **LinkedIn**. It's a new way to network in the post-Covid world beyond the traditional mixer.

The beauty of the 2020s is that LinkedIn has become a place to find your next opportunity or workplace BFF (even if they're at another company or in another country). It's a space for everyone, no matter your experience level. Push past any intimidation or overwhelm if you've never tried it before. Getting comfortable with your personal brand will help your career, elevate your workplace, and put the *power back* in your hands.

LinkedIn is the next evolution in what many of us have been using for the last few decades. Many of us grew up socializing through Myspace, Facebook, and Friendster. Now, sites like Instagram and TikTok help people connect. It's only logical that another social media platform would help us find our professional posse.

Networking doesn't have to be as formal as in years past. It could be as simple as a quick catch-up, message, or comment. From there, the connection can grow into something more meaningful. You can learn from each other and build your network with interesting people.

Shoot your professional shot. If you see someone on LinkedIn whose content resonates, reach out! Slide into their DMs. You don't have to overthink it. It could be as simple as: *"Hey, would you like to meet for a virtual coffee? Would love to learn more about you."* That's how I connected with many fabulous, talented professionals I interviewed for this book.

<u>Almost everyone</u> I reached out to said yes! I reached out to creators whose content I enjoyed. It was a great way to connect with others and make genuine friends. I put aside my fear of rejection or being a "creep" and put myself out there. Some messages get ignored, but some won't. C'est la vie. Reach out and try. It can bloom into an amazing opportunity.

Put your ego aside. Get to know people in your industry and beyond. Get curious. Human connection will always remain in style.

More people will respond than you think—especially if you already developed a connection with them, reacting to and commenting on their posts.

Get a Mentor Or Sponsor—Or Both

Mentors and **sponsors** are additional hype people besides yourself. If you have another person in your organization—especially in a leadership position—advocate for you as a mentor or sponsor, *congratulations*!

They vouch for you, speak positively about you, and communicate your brand when you're not in the room.

What's the difference between a mentor and a sponsor?

- According to Gallup, "A **mentor** shares their knowledge and provides guidance to a less-experienced individual. Anyone with support and advice can provide effective mentorship, regardless of their role or tenure. On the other hand, **sponsors** are in a position of power and actively promote growth by helping provide access to opportunities at work. Sponsors advocate for the career advancement of a less-experienced individual" (Houter & Maese, 2023).

If you can develop a relationship with either a mentor or sponsor—or both—do it. You need someone hyping you up in spaces where you aren't there. Someone who sees the best in you and "gets" you.

Where to start?

Leadership & development coach **Ellen Gills** says, "I love it when companies set up mentoring programs. It's so valuable to help people acclimate. But if they don't have a formal program, it could be worth asking your manager about which leaders they think would be good mentors for you. It's not that you are trying to go around them as your manager, but you are looking for additional voices of support and guidance. You could also ask HR, or ask leaders themselves if they would consider meeting with you once a month or so for connection."

Advocate for yourself by ensuring you're seen the way you want and need to be to evolve in your career. Reach out to people at your organization or beyond that you'd like to get to know better. Maybe they have an interesting hobby or volunteer engagement outside of work. Talk to them. Get to know them. You don't need anyone's permission to be human and get to know people.

Write Your Book

What do you want to say to the world? What's your unique perspective?

Here's some good news! If you want to write a book, you can! Writing a book will help you convey your thought leadership and expertise. "If you'd like to know my approach, read my book!"

Luckily, **publishing is democratized**. You don't have to go from publishing house to publishing house with your manuscript in hand trying to get someone to publish it. **Anyone can publish a book and you can publish it <u>yourself</u>!** That's the beauty of self-publishing, which is how I published this book.

Unexpected layoff? A layoff can be a promotion to author! Instead of freaking out about losing your job, this could be the perfect opportunity to crank out a book in between finding your next job. Go from sad to empowered instantly. Position the book so you can leverage it into other opportunities, whether consulting or speaking. In a competitive and volatile workforce, this is a dramatic way to differentiate your message and value to a prospective employee or client.

Think about your niche and keep this in your back pocket as a backup plan. There are many talented ghostwriters and editors out there who can cheer you on to help you accomplish your goal and cross this bucket list item off your list.

The following are **<u>three options</u> for writing your book**.

Option #1: Write the Book Yourself

It's difficult, stressful, and time-consuming to write the book yourself, but it's doable! You get to say how long it is and what it's about. It's your world.

How can you leverage the book professionally? How do you self-publish?

If writing a book is something you've always wanted to do, you can absolutely do it. You'll just want to do your research. There's a ton of information out there about how to get started, how to self-publish, on how to approach the book development process logically and systematically so you don't overwhelm yourself.

Set standards for yourself but make sure the goals are **realistic and attainable.** At some point, you'll have to call it done and hit the publish button. This is the route I took after getting laid off in the summer of 2023. Writing it was a very grueling process! I initially set a very ambitious goal of finishing the book in 6 weeks, but that was unrealistic and overly optimistic.

You'll want to hire a good editor even (especially) if you write the book yourself. You can also join a mastermind or cohort group for self-publishing writers. And you'll want to make sure you have a good support system (friends, family, colleagues) around you, because it is a challenging journey to go on.

Option #2: Get Support from a Ghostwriter or Book Coach

You don't have to do it alone. There are many talented ghostwriters and book coaches out there who provide various services depending on the level of support you're looking for. On the lighter end, they can help you brainstorm, develop your strategy, and create the steps you need to take to tackle the book yourself. They can also consult with you as you write your book and guide you.

These are mid-way options. This support will help you create a roadmap to follow as you write your book, especially if it's your first time. You don't know what you don't know. Working with an expert who's done it before can help you think of things that may not be on your radar.

Option #3: Partner with a Ghostwriter to Write the Book for You

Do you think Britney Spears and other celebrities who publish books actually write the books themselves? No way. They hire ghostwriters who handle the entire process.

If you select this option, a ghostwriter will take over all writing duties. They will **interview you**. You will then become the subject matter expert and approve the drafts. It's much easier to be interviewed than to write. You just have to be available for meetings and reviews.

And the great news? Depending on your agreement, the ghostwriter does not need writing credit and **you** can receive the full credit as the author. Yes, this is extremely common in the world of ghostwriting.
When you work with a ghostwriter in this option, you can have someone there to walk you through every step of the way. They will capture and express your ideas and thoughts in a way that will resonate.

Take your personal brand to the next level. The world needs to know what you have to offer. Carpe diem.

Takeaways

In this chapter, we learned:

- **Be your own workplace BFF.**
    - Advocate for yourself, what you want, and what you can do. Don't let yourself float in the wind like a plastic bag, à la *American Beauty*.

    - Your positive self-advocacy helps you navigate workplace culture without getting lost in the shuffle or the politics.

- **Direct your career.**
    - Don't just quietly wait for recognition.

    - Personal branding will help you tell your story through content. It shows what you know and can do—whether your current company fully understands that or not. Clarity is key here.

    - Don't assume people will "get" you. Continue to build your brand (also known as your reputation) both online and in person.

- **Use LinkedIn to show your personality and experience.**
    - Celebrate milestones, share lessons learned, and develop your voice and niche throughout your career. This is a platform available to every professional!

- **Network!**
  - ○ Connect with other professionals by commenting, messaging, and communicating through LinkedIn.

  - ○ LinkedIn is the new way to network with professionals around the globe and make your voice known rather than waiting for formal networking events at the Chamber of Commerce.

  - ○ It's a great way to develop your professional community and make IRL friends.

- **Advocate for YOU.**
  - ○ No one will advocate for you the way you will *advocate for yourself.*

  - ○ Believe in yourself first and foremost, rather than waiting for someone to discover or sponsor you.

  - ○ Share that message with others and get them on board, especially mentors or sponsors. They'll advocate for you when you're not around.

- **Write your book!**
  - ○ *Got laid off?* Congratulations! You've been promoted to the position of author. You can write your book anytime. Here are your three options to bring your book to life.

    1. **Write it yourself.**
       This is a free option, yet the most stressful and time-consuming. You will want to hire an editor to ensure there are no errors and it makes sense to the reader.

    2. **Get support from a ghostwriter or book coach.**
       They can help with the brainstorming and outlining of the book. The costs would be more than nothing but less than the full package.

    3. **Partner with a ghostwriter to write the book for you.**
       This is the most costly option, but it is an investment in your career and personal brand. Make sure you research your message, industry, and how you want to leverage the book into consulting or speaking engagements. Once you've written it, you have it forever! Invest in yourself. Empower yourself and position your personal brand how you want it.

Self-Reflection Activity

Pretend you are someone else. See yourself as a best friend who is explaining you to someone else. You are proud of your friend and think the world of them and their abilities. Now, reflect on how you can be your own workplace BFF.

Q: *How would I describe myself professionally?*
Tip: List your roles, skills, and passions. What are the common themes?

_____

_____

_____

_____

_____

_____

_____

_____

_____

_____

_____

_____

_____

_____

_____

_____

_____

_____

_____

_____

_____

_____

Q: Looking at the previous question, what is my *30-second professional elevator pitch?* Write it out. Now practice it. Record it. Play it back. Embrace the awkwardness.

_____

_____

_____

_____

_____

_____

_____

_____

_____

_____

_____

_____

_____

_____

_____

_____

_____

_____

_____

_____

_____

_____

_____

_____

_____

_____

Q: *What do people naturally come to me for?*
Movie recommendations? Excel tips? **Tip:** Ask
friends for more insight. Cross out anything that
feels uncomfortable sharing with others. For
everything else, create a 2-line post for LinkedIn to
test out this week.

_____
_____
_____
_____
_____
_____
_____
_____
_____
_____
_____
_____
_____
_____
_____
_____
_____
_____
_____
_____
_____
_____
_____
_____

Q: *What do I want to do in my career that I haven't been able to do yet?* How do I want to be seen that I haven't yet?

_____
_____
_____
_____
_____
_____
_____
_____
_____
_____
_____
_____
_____
_____
_____
_____
_____
_____
_____
_____
_____
_____
_____
_____
_____
_____
_____
_____
_____

Q: *Who is my mentor or sponsor?* If not, who can I reach out to for mentorship or sponsorship? Who seems interesting that I'd like to get to know? **Tip:** List a few people to reach out to develop new connections outside of your comfort zone.

_____
_____
_____
_____
_____
_____
_____
_____
_____
_____
_____
_____
_____
_____
_____
_____
_____
_____
_____
_____
_____
_____
_____
_____
_____
_____
_____
_____
_____

Q: *What would I write a book about?* Tip: List a few ideas and how you can leverage the book.

_____

_____

_____

_____

_____

_____

_____

_____

_____

_____

_____

_____

_____

_____

_____

_____

_____

_____

_____

_____

_____

_____

_____

_____

_____

_____

_____

_____

_____

_____

_____

Conclusion

Personal/professional development is a metamorphosis. The journey is much more unstructured—*and unhinged*—than the more straightforward trajectory you were accustomed to in school. If you showed up and did the work in school, you got good grades. The workplace is complex.

Just like the colorful and delicious children's tale *The Very Hungry Caterpillar* by Eric Carle, *developing yourself* can resemble the journey of an insatiable caterpillar who nibbles through an assortment of food before finally transforming into a **beautiful butterfly**. The caterpillar needed all the apples and cakes and pickles to get enough nutrients to fuel its transformation.

And *fun fact*: During metamorphosis, a caterpillar disintegrates all of its tissues except for "imaginal cells" or discs to become a butterfly. The disintegrated tissue fuels the rapid cell division required to form the butterfly. The remaining imaginal cells remain, and the butterfly actually can *remember* its pre-butterfly life as a caterpillar (Jabr, 2012).

Just like a butterfly, you remember your **workplace metamorphosis**. Think of how far you've come. Some of us may be tempted to wipe our memories clean of traumatic workplace memories, but *what was the point of it all if you can't remember and learn from it?* Keep your imaginal cells as you transform and remember where you've been and where you want to go.

It's all part of the process. Like the hungry caterpillar gobbling up treats, all the "food" (*development, growth, and resources*) you consume in your workplace journey ultimately nourishes your development. You needed it. It taught you. It nourished you. Even the bad experiences fed you and got you ready for your transformation.

TAKEAWAY MESSAGE
Growth is change. Embrace it!

Your career journey will be very different than you originally thought. And that's okay! Most people can say their career journey is not what they imagined it would be. Life is unpredictable—there's no way you can have a nice and neat career journey with no bumps and redirects.

It's hard to predict where your career will go next with so many *unknown* unknowns and different personalities and dynamics around you. YOU will be very different from the beginning of the journey to the middle to the end. Everything you experience is ultimately fueling your journey and evolution in life. And that's the beauty of the journey.

When you are open to **growing, learning, and evolving**, it doesn't impact just you alone; it also impacts the collective. While personal growth can start in the workplace, taking that growth and reflecting on the topics in this book will give you a roadmap for enlightenment. This fuels your professional development and prepares you for the next steps in your career. And it will ultimately elevate your level of consciousness.

As Bob Marley, reggae icon and international symbol of love and peace, sang, **"None but ourselves can free our mind."**

Personal development isn't just another thing you "should" do in a drowning self-care checklist. It's about consistently fine-tuning consciousness throughout your lifetime to be the best professional/partner/parent/friend/family member/community member you can be.

It's an openness to do better. It's a willingness to examine things from a different lens.

It's about being **as whole as you can be** in the spaces you occupy.

Many people know the right things that they need to do or should do, but it's the lens through which you see the world and how you incorporate those changes that make all the difference.

It's the stories you tell yourself. The way you speak to yourself. The way you interact with others.

In summary, let's recall what you learned in this book.

In this book, there are 6 personal development lessons to help you navigate <u>any</u> workplace.

1 Be aware of your surroundings.

2 Journey into your awareness.

3 Improve your communication.

4 Understand your conflict style.

5 Manage your expectations.

6 Be your own workplace BFF.

Remember, the workplace is a mirror of the world. And it's in a transformational shift right now. Self-discovery—brought on by workplace development—really has the opportunity to heal and evolve us on a deeper level than just professionally. And remember, you have more power than you may know. When you change, the spaces you occupy change as well.

You're cool enough to be open and curious about learning and growing. And you're *even cooler* now that you've read this book, reflected in the exercises, and manifested ways that you can create more of what you want to see in the world. Practice what you've learned. You can always return to the exercises at any time and update the answers as needed.

Want more opportunity? Create it. *Want more kindness?* Model it.

Good luck elevating the vibration and creating the reality you want to see by working on yourself and shifting the workplace—and world—in a better direction. It's been my pleasure to guide you through this valley of personal and professional development, introspection, and vibration elevation.

Go out there and share your coolness with the world. Elevate the vibration of your spaces.

Follow me on LinkedIn for exclusive offers for readers of this book and let's keep the "Be Cool" journey going together. Use the hashtag #everybodybecool and post your thoughts or a photo of you with the book. Visit everybody-be-cool for more information.

Thank you, thank you, thank you (as the great Fozzie Bear of *Muppets* fame would say) for doing this work. *Wakka wakka!*

Power to the workplace butterflies!

Next Steps: Your Personal/Professional Development Journey

Now that you've read the entire book, keep the personal/professional development plan going. Development is, after all, a lifelong journey.

Go back and review the takeaways from each lesson as well as your answers from the self-reflective exercises. Determine what you can do to implement these lessons.

In the section below, fill out the actionable steps you will take to take control of your career in the next 30/60/90 days.

Make it doable. Make it fun. Make it you.

This is **your plan**—no one else's.

30 Day Plan

---

60 Day Plan

_____

_____

_____

_____

_____

_____

_____

_____

_____

_____

_____

_____

_____

_____

_____

_____

_____

_____

_____

_____

_____

_____

90 Day Plan

About the Author

Hanan Harb Sahourieh joined the workplace in the early 2000s. As an avid pop culture buff who grew up watching classic workplace movies like *9 to 5* and *Office Space*, Hanan's fascination with the workplace began in childhood.

After graduating college with a degree in English literature and psychology, Hanan developed her niche in the actual workplace in writing, marketing, and learning roles.

During her time in the learning & development industry, Hanan noticed how many elements of spirituality and personal development were incorporated into professional and leadership development programs.

She became passionate about making these tools and resources available to the _entire_ workforce so that everyone could benefit (and not just leaders). That's where *Everybody, Be Cool* was born.

Her works have appeared in publications such as *Artvoice*, *eLearning Industry*, *Training Industry*, and *Training* magazines.

Hanan's Workplace Matters newsletter gained thousands of followers on LinkedIn, earning her the nickname "Your Workplace BFF."

In addition to being an author, Hanan is a professional development consultant and ghostwriter. Her creative strategy combines marketing, content, and learning best practices.

Hanan is a mom, partner, yoga enthusiast, and lifelong Buffalo Bills fan.

She enjoys strolling through nature, exploring libraries, and examining fresh produce.

Go to everybody-be-cool.com to learn more.

References

The 7 Habits of Highly Effective People®. (n.d.). FranklinCovey. Retrieved February 4, 2024, from https://www.franklincovey.com/the-7-habits/

Achter, P. J. (2024, March 21). *McCarthyism | Definition, History, & Facts*. Britannica. Retrieved August 3, 2023, from https://www.britannica.com/event/McCarthyism

AMNH. (n.d.). *Beyond Our Lizard Brain | AMNH*. American Museum of Natural History. Retrieved November 20, 2023, from https://www.amnh.org/exhibitions/brain-the-inside-story/your-emotional-brain/beyond-our-lizard-brain

Armstrong, J. (Executive Producer). (2018). *Succession* [TV series]. HBO.

Atlassian.com. (2020). *A 2020 Retrospective on the History of Work - Infographic*. Atlassian. Retrieved August 29, 2023, from https://www.atlassian.com/history-of-work

Ayn Rand Institute (ARI). (n.d.). Welcome to Ayn Rand Institute - AynRand.org. Retrieved August 20, 2023, from https://aynrand.org/

Baldwin, J. (1970). *James Baldwin | Love has never been a Popular Movement*. YouTube. Retrieved November 2, 2023, from https://www.youtube.com/watch?v=6xpE2-IGPy8

Bariso, J. (2019, September 30). 28 Emotional Intelligence Quotes That Can Help Make Emotions Work for You, Instead of Against You. *Inc. Magazine*. https://www.inc.com/justin-bariso/28-emotional-intelligence-quotes-that-can-help-make-emotions-work-for-you-instead-of-against-you.html

Bavin, E. (2023, 2 March). *'We're like family' and other workplace red flags*. Yahoo Finance. Retrieved October 23, 2024, from https://au.finance.yahoo.com/news/were-like-family-and-other-workplace-red-flags-003213336.html?guccounter=1&guce_referrer=aHR0cHM6Ly93d3cuZ29vZ2xl

LmNvbS8&guce_referrer_sig=AQAAABIVYTtr_HsdI5EhUkX7yb9ZL02lb0I3kYco

aEhZv5FNza0c1n1YmXQ4CGeWWgXNxtz46q_bGpmI2r

Bersin, J. (2019, October 31). *Let's Stop Talking About Soft Skills: They're PowerSkills.*
Josh Bersin. Retrieved December 8, 2023, from
https://joshbersin.com/2019/10/lets-stop-talking-about-soft-skills-theyre-power-ski
lls/

BetterUp. (n.d.). *Better Up.* Wikipedia. Retrieved September 18, 2023, from
https://grow.betterup.com/resources/coaching-culture-insights-report?_gl=1*14k0
5iy*_gcl_au*MzYyMDU2NjI3LjE2OTU4NDcwODA.

BetterUp. (n.d.). *Insights Report.* Wikipedia. Retrieved September 20, 2023, from
https://grow.betterup.com/resources/coaching-culture-insights-report?_gl=1*14k0
5iy*_gcl_au*MzYyMDU2NjI3LjE2OTU4NDcwODA.#footer

Brown, B. (2012, March 16). *Brené Brown: Listening to shame.* TED. Retrieved December
21, 2023, from
https://www.ted.com/talks/brene_brown_listening_to_shame?language=en

Budson, A. (2017, December 3). Don't Listen to Your Lizard Brain. *Psychology Today.*
https://www.psychologytoday.com/us/blog/managing-your-memory/201712/don-t-
listen-your-lizard-brain

Bureau of Labor. (2022, September 22). *Employee Tenure in 2022.* Bureau of Labor
Statistics. Retrieved February 3, 2024, from
https://www.bls.gov/news.release/pdf/tenure.pdf

Carnegie, D. (1998). *How to Win Friends & Influence People.* Pocket Books.

Carucci, R. (2023, December 5). How Leaders Fake Psychological Safety. *Harvard
Business Review.* https://hbr.org/2023/12/how-leaders-fake-psychological-safety

Carucci, R. (2023, December 5). How Leaders Fake Psychological Safety. *Harvard
Business Review.* https://hbr.org/2023/12/how-leaders-fake-psychological-safety

Chase, D. (Executive Producer). (1999-2007). *The Sopranos* [TV series]. HBO.

Cold War | Summary, Causes, History, Years, Timeline, & Facts. (n.d.). Britannica.

Retrieved July 29, 2023, from https://www.britannica.com/event/Cold-War

Connelly, Mosher, Conway (Executive Producer). (1957). *Leave it to Beaver* [TV series].

Crucial Conversations. (n.d.). *Crucial Conversations - Free Book Resources*. Crucial

Learning. Retrieved December 12, 2023, from

https://cruciallearning.com/crucial-conversations-book/

DiSC. (n.d.). *DiSC*. Everything DiSC Official Site | Everything Disc. Retrieved December 8,

2023, from https://www.everythingdisc.com/

Drake Baer. (2014, April 23). A Brief History of How the Cubicle. *Business Insider*.

https://www.businessinsider.com/a-brief-history-of-how-the-cubicle-2014-4

Durkheim, É. (n.d.). *Collective conscience*. Oxford Reference. Retrieved September 6,

2023, from

https://www.oxfordreference.com/display/10.1093/oi/authority.201108030956239

83

Enneagram. (n.d.). *The Nine Enneagram Type Descriptions*. The Enneagram Institute.

Retrieved April 8, 2024, from

https://www.enneagraminstitute.com/type-descriptions

Eurich, T. (2018, January 4). *What Self-Awareness Really Is (and How to Cultivate It)*.

Harvard Business Review. Retrieved September 10, 2023, from

https://hbr.org/2018/01/what-self-awareness-really-is-and-how-to-cultivate-it

Executive Coaching | Executive Leadership Coaching | CCL. (n.d.). Ccl.org. Retrieved

December 18, 2023, from

https://www.ccl.org/leadership-solutions/leadership-coaching/executive-coaching/

Farley, M. (2023, August 16). *Volume 18 - by Meredith Farley - Content People*. Meredith

Farley | Substack. Retrieved August 25, 2023, from

https://meredithfarley.substack.com/p/volume-18

Fincher, D. (Director). (2010). *The Social Network* [Film]. Columbia Pictures, Relativity

Media.

Foley, J. (Director). (1992). *Glengarry Glen Ross* [Film]. Zupnik Enterprises.

Frankel, D. (Director). (2006). *The Devil Wears Prada* [Film]. Fox 2000 Pictures.

Friedan, B. (2001). *The Feminine Mystique*. W. W. Norton & Company.
    https://www.amazon.com/Feminine-Mystique-Betty-Friedan/dp/0393322572

Gallup. (2023, August 24). *Getting Your Work Culture Right*. Gallup.com. Retrieved July 11,
    2023, from
    https://www.gallup.com/workplace/508904/getting-work-culture-right.aspx

Gervais, R. (Executive Producer). (2005-2013). *The Office* [TV series]. NBC Universal
    Television Studio.

Gibran, K. (n.d.). *Khalil Gibran Quote: "The tiny flame that lights up the human heart is like
    a blazing torch that comes down from heaven to light up the paths ..."*
    QuoteFancy. Retrieved February 2, 2024, from
    https://quotefancy.com/quote/848226/Khalil-Gibran-The-tiny-flame-that-lights-up-t
    he-human-heart-is-like-a-blazing-torch-that

Gibson, L. C. (2023). *Disentangling from Emotionally Immature People: Avoid Emotional
    Traps, Stand Up for Your Self, and Transform Your Relationships as an Adult
    Child of Emotionally Immature Parents*. New Harbinger Publications.

Goldstein, K. (2018, December 6). Lean In, Sheryl Sandberg, and the "feminist" advice that
    failed me. *Vox*.
    https://www.vox.com/first-person/2018/12/6/18128838/michelle-obama-lean-in-sh
    eryl-sandberg

Goleman, D. (2005). *Emotional Intelligence: Why It Can Matter More Than IQ*. Random
    House Publishing Group.

Greene, R. (2000). *The 48 laws of power*. Penguin Publishing Group.

Greenleaf, R. K. (2002). *Servant Leadership: A Journey into the Nature of Legitimate
    Power and Greatness 25th Anniversary Edition*. Paulist Press.
    https://www.amazon.com/Servant-Leadership-Legitimate-Greatness-Anniversary/
    dp/0809105543/ref=sr_1_1?crid=2FRSGS0GVZF4U&dib=eyJ2IjoiMSJ9.ZEpKP4

8M1ChVuXBcfAO5AGuEqkGP8ym4xWdVs8SKsy-5uuYayxkyvc-R5z-VIUHhiv2Et

Ygfe6wMEGJZkO5zY83DUJDbtoNcPfm3lv6EqLX9XQ6uRrMslaiO

Grenny, J., Patterson, K., McMillan, R., Switzler, A., & Gregory, E. (2021). *Crucial Conversations: Tools for Talking When Stakes are High, Third Edition.* McGraw-Hill Education.

Grundhoefer, L. (2023, October 5). Move Over, Millennials — Here's How Gen Alpha's Top Entrepreneurs Are Printing Money. *Entrepreneur.* https://www.entrepreneur.com/starting-a-business/move-over-millennials-how-gen-alphas-top-entrepreneurs/462793?utm_source=creator-reports.beehiiv.com&utm_medium=newsletter&utm_campaign=virtual-influencers

Haden, J. (2019, September 4). Warren Buffett and Bill Gates Still Say This Is the Best Business Book Ever Written. *Inc. Magazine.* https://www.inc.com/jeff-haden/warren-buffett-bill-gates-still-say-this-is-best-business-book-ever-written.html

Hamlin, R. (2024, March 8). *Civil rights | Definition, Types, Activists, History, & Facts.* Britannica. Retrieved January 4, 2024, from https://www.britannica.com/topic/civil-rights

Headspace. (n.d.). *Meditations You Can Do At Work.* Headspace. Retrieved December 20, 2023, from https://www.headspace.com/meditation/work-meditation

Herek, S. (Director). (1991). *Don't Tell Mom the Babysitter's Dead* [Film]. Warner Brothers.

Herek, S. (Director). (1996). *101 Dalmatians* [Film]. Walt Disney Pictures.

Higgins, C. (Director). (1980). *9 to 5* [Film]. IPC Films.

Holiday, R. (2016). *Ego Is the Enemy.* Penguin Publishing Group.

Houter, K. D., & Maese, E. (2023, April 13). *Mentors and Sponsors Make the Difference.* Gallup.com. Retrieved April 8, 2024, from https://www.gallup.com/workplace/473999/mentors-sponsors-difference.aspx

Hughes, A. (2017, June 27). *4 Methods to Mastering Your 'Monkey Mind'*. Yogapedia. Retrieved December 5, 2023, from https://www.yogapedia.com/2/7051/self/how-to-master-your-mind

Jabr, F. (2012, August 10). How Does a Caterpillar Turn into a Butterfly? *Scientific American.* https://www.scientificamerican.com/article/caterpillar-butterfly-metamorphosis-explainer/

Jackson, J. (2021). *Unlock Your Conscious Leadership: Liberate Your Four Key Parts: Mind, Heart, Body, and Talent.* Independently published.

Jaques, E. (2001). *Changing Culture of a Factory.* Routledge. https://www.amazon.com/Changing-International-Behavioural-Sciences-Tavistock /dp/0415264421

Jon Kabat-Zinn. (2024). Jon Kabat-Zinn: Home. Retrieved January 5, 2024, from https://jonkabat-zinn.com/

Judge, M. (Director). (1999). *Office Space* [Film]. 20th Century Fox.

Kornhaber, S., & Beck, J. (2019, August 25). Succession 'Hunting': The Meaning of Boar on the Floor. *The Atlantic.* https://www.theatlantic.com/entertainment/archive/2019/08/succession-hunting-review-meaning-boar-on-the-floor/596584/

Legal Highlight: The Civil Rights Act of 1964. (n.d.). U.S. Department of Labor. Retrieved January 4, 2024, from https://www.dol.gov/agencies/oasam/civil-rights-center/statutes/civil-rights-act-of-1964

Leiba, E. (2022). *I'm Not Yelling: A Black Woman's Guide to Navigating the Workplace.* Mango Media.

Lencioni, P. (2009). *The Five Dysfunctions Of A Team.* Wiley India Pvt. Limited.

Loria, K. (2023, May 29). Here's which generation you are... *Business Insider*.

https://www.businessinsider.com/generation-you-are-in-by-birth-year-millennial-g

en-x-baby-boomer-2018-3

Love Serve Remember Foundation. (2024). *Episode 14 - Meditation*. Love Serve

Remember Foundation. Retrieved January 4, 2024, from

https://www.ramdass.org/meditation-3/

Lumet, S. (Director). (1976). *Network* [Film]. Metro-Goldwyn-Mayer.

MacLaury, J. (n.d.). *Government Regulation of Workers' Safety and Health, 1877-1917*.

U.S. Department of Labor. Retrieved August 15, 2023, from

https://www.dol.gov/general/aboutdol/history/mono-regsafeintrotoc

Many contributors. (2023, July 2). *How to Create Your Own Personal Brand Voice*.

LinkedIn. Retrieved February 7, 2024, from

https://www.linkedin.com/advice/0/how-can-you-create-your-own-personal-brand-

voice

Markish, J. (2023, January 25). *How to Promote Psychological Safety With HR Tools*.

Lattice. Retrieved August 13, 2023, from

https://lattice.com/library/how-to-promote-psychological-safety-with-hr-tools

Maté, G., & Maté, D. (2022). *The Myth of Normal: Trauma, Illness, and Healing in a Toxic

Culture*. Penguin Publishing Group.

Maté M.D., G. (2011). *When the Body Says No: Exploring the Stress-Disease Connection*.

Wiley.

McKay, A. (Director). (2015). *The Big Short* [Film]. Regency Enterprises, Plan B

Entertainment.

McKinsey. (2023, January 13). *2023 DEI initiatives report: Inside the lighthouses*. McKinsey

& Company. Retrieved January 5, 2024, from

https://www.mckinsey.com/featured-insights/diversity-and-inclusion/diversity-equit

y-and-inclusion-lighthouses-2023

Mcleod, S. (n.d.). *Maslow's Hierarchy of Needs*. Simply Psychology. Retrieved August 4,

2024, from https://www.simplypsychology.org/maslow.html

Mendes, S. (Director). (1999). *American Beauty* [Film]. Jinks/Cohen Company.

Merriam-Webster. (n.d.). *Empathy Definition & Meaning*. Merriam-Webster. Retrieved

August 11, 2023, from https://www.merriam-webster.com/dictionary/empathy

Mind Tools. (n.d.). *Empathic Listening - Going Beyond Active Listening*. Mind Tools.

Retrieved January 15, 2024, from

https://www.mindtools.com/a8l9j08/empathic-listening

Morse, G. (2006). Decisions and Desire. *Harvard Business Review*.

https://hbr.org/2006/01/decisions-and-desire

Narvaez, D. F. (2021, January 10). *Understanding the Integrated Brain*. Psychology Today.

Retrieved November 1, 2023, from

https://www.psychologytoday.com/us/blog/moral-landscapes/202101/understandi

ng-the-integrated-brain

O'Brien, J. (2023, October 30). Why Erika Jayne's Lack of Empathy Is Extremely Troubling

(But Not Surprising). *Yahoo*.

https://www.yahoo.com/entertainment/why-erika-jayne-lack-empathy-185926573.

html

Perry, E. (2023, March 14). *Favoritism in the Workplace: How to Manage It*. BetterUp.

Retrieved November 13, 2023, from

https://www.betterup.com/blog/favoritism-in-workplace

Pomerance, M. (2021, March 2). *What Role Do You Play In Your Family System? — The

Candidly*. The Candidly. Retrieved September 8, 2023, from

https://www.thecandidly.com/2019/what-role-do-you-play-in-your-family-system-of

-origin

The Predictive Index. (n.d.). *The PI Behavioral Assessment Test For Employment*. The

Predictive Index. Retrieved January 22, 2024, from

https://www.predictiveindex.com/assessments/behavioral-assessment/

Quotes. (n.d.). *Bob Marley Quotes - BrainyQuote*. Brainy Quote. Retrieved April 8, 2024,

    from https://www.brainyquote.com/authors/bob-marley-quotes

Raab, D. (2017, September 13). Calming the Monkey Mind. *Psychology Today*.

    https://www.psychologytoday.com/us/blog/the-empowerment-diary/201709/calmi

    ng-the-monkey-mind

Rogers, F. M. (Executive Producer). (1968-2001). *Mister Rogers' Neighborhood* [TV series].

    WQED Studios.

Sandberg, S., & Scovell, N. (2013). *Lean In: Women, Work, and the Will to Lead*. Knopf

    Doubleday Publishing Group.

Sanok, J. (2022, April 14). A Guide to Setting Better Boundaries. *Harvard Business Review*.

    https://hbr.org/2022/04/a-guide-to-setting-better-boundaries

Santomero, A. C. (Executive Producer). (2012 - Present). *Daniel Tiger's Neighborhood* [TV

    series]. Fred Rogers Productions.

Shakespeare, W. (2003). *Macbeth (Folger Shakespeare Library)*. Simon & Schuster.

    https://www.amazon.com/Macbeth-Folger-Shakespeare-Library-William/dp/07434

    77103/ref=asc_df_0743477103/?tag=hyprod-20&linkCode=df0&hvadid=3121320

    76929&hvpos=&hvnetw=g&hvrand=5122758830564893890&hvpone=&hvptwo=

    &hvqmt=&hvdev=c&hvdvcmdl=&hvlocint=&hvlocphy=101

Shoss, M. (2023, May 12). Employers need to focus on workplace burnout: Here's why.

    American Psychological Association.

    https://www.apa.org/topics/healthy-workplaces/workplace-burnout

Silverstein, S. (1999). *The Giving Tree (Slipcased Mini Edition)*. HarperCollins.

    https://www.amazon.com/Giving-Tree-Shel-Silverstein/dp/006028451X

Sinclair, U. (2019). *The Jungle*. CreateSpace Independent Publishing Platform.

Smith, S. (2018, April 10). *BHP Blog - Behavioral Health Partners (BHP)*. BHP Blog -

    Behavioral Health Partners (BHP) - University of Rochester Medical Center.

    Retrieved January 8, 2024, from

https://www.urmc.rochester.edu/behavioral-health-partners/bhp-blog/april-2018/5-
4-3-2-1-coping-technique-for-anxiety.aspx

Smithsonian. (n.d.). *Work*. Smithsonian American Women's History Museum.
https://womenshistory.si.edu/herstory/work

Stiller, B. (Director). (1994). *Reality Bites* [Film]. Universal Pictures.

The World Economic Forum. (2022, May 19). *Gen Z don't want to work for you. Here's how
to fix that*. The World Economic Forum. Retrieved October 18, 2023, from
https://www.weforum.org/agenda/2022/05/gen-z-don-t-want-to-work-for-you-here-
s-how-to-change-their-mind/

Tolle, E. (2004). *The Power of Now*. Namaste Pub.

Tyson, N. D. (n.d.). *Quote by Neil DeGrasse Tyson: "We are all connected; To each other,
biological..."* Goodreads. Retrieved September 4, 2023, from
https://www.goodreads.com/quotes/387320-we-are-all-connected-to-each-other-b
iologically-to-the

Vibration Definition & Meaning. (n.d.). Merriam-Webster. Retrieved January 4, 2024, from
https://www.merriam-webster.com/dictionary/vibration

WHO. (n.d.). *Mental health*. World Health Organization (WHO). Retrieved November 20,
2023, from https://www.who.int/health-topics/mental-health#tab=tab_1

Yogananda, P. (2021). *Autobiography of a Yogi*. Self-Realization Fellowship.
https://www.amazon.com/Autobiography-of-Yogi-Ben-Kingsley-audiobook/dp/B00
06IU7LS/ref=sr_1_3?crid=29WQ75GL2QALA&dib=eyJ2IjoiMSJ9.IWNDJWn4_9
Bb-0Ybl4QI_1blxrpMcxFSq6E7Kpg4_L5dyWimQzsRlRZxsg9kMeXZQOugNUcx7
Nzx0oq1cJ6oDOW2JUSrGPF_VtYbCpiKpUP9oQo1SvIUDyHd5Q6A2yf

Younger, B. (Director). (2000). *Boiler Room* [Film]. Team Todd.

Zinn, H. (n.d.). *Quotes by Howard Zinn (Author of A People's History of the United States)*.
Goodreads. Retrieved September 2, 2023, from
https://www.goodreads.com/author/quotes/1899.Howard_Zinn

Zinn, H. (1995). *A People's History of the United States*. Harper Perennial Modern Classics.

FIN

Milton Keynes UK
Ingram Content Group UK Ltd.
UKHW022136130524
442624UK00008B/37